THE LANGUAGE OF
SYMBOLS

THE LANGUAGE OF
SYMBOLS

A VISUAL KEY TO SYMBOLS AND THEIR MEANINGS

DAVID FONTANA

ILLUSTRATIONS BY HANNAH FIRMIN

DUNCAN BAIRD PUBLISHERS

LONDON

The Language of Symbols
David Fontana

This edition first published in the United
Kingdom and Ireland in 2003 by Duncan Baird
Publishers Ltd
Sixth Floor, Castle House
75–76 Wells Street
London W1T 3QH

Conceived, edited and designed by Duncan Baird Publishers Ltd.

First published in Great Britain in 1993 by Pavilion Books
Limited, 26 Upper Ground, London SE1 9PD.

Editor: Peter Bently
Designer: Gail Jones
Managing Editor: Christopher Westhorp
Managing Designer: Manisha Patel
Commissioned Artwork: Hannah Firmin/Sharp Practice
Picture Researcher: Julia Brown

British Library Cataloguing-in-Publication Data:
A catalogue record for this book is available from the British
Library

ISBN: 1-904292-25-9

10 9 8 7 6 5 4 3 2 1

Main text typeset in Garamond
Colour reproduction by Colourscan, Singapore
Printed and bound in Singapore by Imago

NOTES
The abbreviations BCE and CE are used throughout this book:
BCE Before the Common Era (the equivalent of BC)
CE Common Era (the equivalent of AD)
Any uncaptioned images are described on page 320.

CONTENTS

Introduction	8
The Jungian View	13
The Archetypes	18
Cultural Perspectives	25
THE POWER OF SYMBOLS	30
Symbols in Prehistory	32
Gods and Myths	38
Ritual, Magic and Prayer	44
Male and Female	49
Opposition and Unity	52
Cross-currents	56
THE USES OF SYMBOLS	60
Symbols in Art	63
The Search for Inner Wisdom	71
Dream Symbols	75
THE WORLD OF SYMBOLS	84
SHAPES AND COLOURS	87
Sacred Geometry	90
Mandalas and Yantras	99
Mazes and Labyrinths	102
Numbers and Sounds	104
Colours	108

OBJECTS	111
Royalty, Office and Consecration	114
War and Peace	118
Musical Instruments	122
Knots, Cords and Rings	124
Buildings and Monuments	126
ANIMALS	129
Dragons and Serpents	132
Heraldic Beasts	137
Dogs, Foxes and Wolves	139
Cats	141
Birds and Flight	143
Fishes and Shells	146
Monkeys and Elephants	149
Sheep and Goats	151
Bulls, Stags and Bears	153
Swine	155
Lesser Creatures	157
Hybrid Creatures	159
THE NATURAL WORLD	164
Trees	167
Flowers and Plants	173
Food and Drink	176
The Elements	180
Rainbows	192
Thunder and Lightning	194
Day and Night	196
Jewels and Precious Metals	198
Sun, Moon and Stars	201

Contents

HUMAN AND SPIRITUAL SYMBOLS	205
Sex and Fertility	208
Body, Youth and Age	211
Good and Evil	216
Haloes, Masks and Shadows	218
Gods and Goddesses	222
Witches, Priests and Wizards	228
Heaven and Hell	230
SYMBOL SYSTEMS	236
Occult Systems	242
Alchemy	246
The Kabbalah	255
Astrology	263
The Tarot	282
Working with the Tarot	286
Tantra	303
The *Yijing*	307
Glossary	312
Index	314
Acknowledgments	320

Contents

INTRODUCTION

Symbols are profound expressions of human nature and occur in all cultures at all times. From their first appearance in Paleolithic caves, they have accompanied the development of civilization, and in their correct context they still speak powerfully to our intellect, emotions and spirit.

Human communication depends largely on signs in the form of written or spoken words, images or gestures. These symbols are conscious and explicit representations of reality – of objects, actions and concepts in the world around us. But there is another aspect of symbolism that is equally important though less explicit: the side that relates to our inner psychological and spiritual world. Within this inner world, a symbol can represent some deep intuitive wisdom that eludes direct expression. Older civilizations recognized the power of symbols and used

Introduction

them extensively in their art, religions, myths and rituals. Although they are often dismissed by Western rationalism, the inner significance of symbols is undiminished today, and they still appear frequently in art, literature and film, and in the stories loved by successive generations of children. Deep-rooted symbols are used subliminally and cynically in advertisements, and even in political campaigns. Most people confront the profoundest symbols in dreams; they are also seen in the spontaneous paintings and drawings of children and of patients in psychotherapy.

According to the Swiss psychologist and psychotherapist Carl Jung, symbols generate themselves from the unconscious as a spontaneous expression of some deep inner power of which we are aware but which we cannot fully express in words. Certain kinds of symbolism constitute a universal language, because the images and their meanings occur in similar forms – and carry similar power – across cultures and centuries. The symbols that go to make

Introduction

up this language are the natural expression of inner psychological forces.

Perhaps because of an intuitive awareness of the part they play in our inner lives, people tend to be drawn to symbols. Drawing upon psychology, Eastern and Western spirituality, anthropology and history, this book aims to respond to this interest and provide easy access to the symbolic world.

HIEROGLYPHS
Egyptian "sacred script" is made up of stylized images of natural or artificial objects. Some convey meaning and others have phonetic value.

EMBLEMS
Symbols, like the Christian three fishes in this 15th-century painting, are central to the medieval science of heraldry.

THE JUNGIAN VIEW

Modern theories about the meanings and uses of symbols are derived largely from the pioneering work of Carl Gustav Jung (1875–1961). In analyzing the dreams of various patients – normal, neurotic and psychotic – Jung noted the recurrence of certain deeply symbolic images, such as the mandala (see pages 99–101). He was also struck by the similarity between the images that emerged during analysis and the symbols appearing in Eastern and Western religions, myths, legends and rituals, particularly those of esoteric movements such as alchemy (see pages 246–254). Jung concluded not only that some symbols are of universal significance, but also that symbolism plays an important part in the psychic processes

JUNG AND THE ALCHEMISTS
Jung believed that alchemical symbols could be powerful expressions of the collective unconscious.

The Jungian View

that influence every aspect of human thought and endeavour.

Jung believed the human psyche – the sum of conscious and unconscious mental activity – to have a real and discernible structure. Consciousness comprises the thoughts and actions under the control of the will. It is underlaid by the "preconscious", the mental faculties and memories which can be readily summoned into consciousness, and by the "personal unconscious", a vast reservoir of individual memories (perceptions, experiences and repressed desires) to which we occasionally gain access as they surface into consciousness through dreams or sudden flashes of recollection. Buried still deeper in the human psyche, in Jung's view, is the "collective unconscious", the seat of those instinctive patterns of thought and behaviour shaped by millennia of human experience into what we now recognize as emotions and values. These primordial images cannot be called up into consciousness: they can only be examined in symbolic form, personalized as men or women, or as images projected by our minds onto the outside world. Jung called these primordial symbols "archetypes" and saw them as the common inheritance of humankind.

According to Jung, an individual is psychologically "healthy" when the conscious and unconscious minds are in dynamic balance. He held that psychic energy (the "life-force") flowed from the unconscious to the conscious to satisfy the demands of the conscious mind, and in the reverse direction to satisfy the unconscious mind. Any interruption of this progression or regression is a failure to reconcile the opposing forces that make up the human psyche, and leads to inner conflict. As well as the division between the conscious and the unconscious, these forces consist of other "opposites", such as intuition and rationality, emotion and thought, instincts and spirituality, and the various paired

The Jungian View

aspects of the personality such as extroversion and introversion, mastery and sympathy, and negativity and conformity. Jung's belief that archetypal symbols can be used to explore the boundaries between the conscious and unconscious mind had an important influence on his clinical techniques. He analyzed the symbols in the dreams of his patients, seeing them as vital clues to their psychological problems and as indicators of their progress. Jung's techniques are widely used in psychotherapy today: for example, a patient may be encouraged to meditate upon a symbol, or to provide words associated with it, in an attempt to unlock its meaning. Once the meaning becomes clear, the patient not only obtains new insights into his or her own mind, but usually finds that meaningful symbols begin to occur with greater and greater frequency, as if each symbol unlocks a door into the unconscious through which other symbols are then allowed to emerge.

It was largely because of his ideas on symbolism that Jung was forced to break with his friend and mentor, Sigmund Freud. Freud also attached great importance to the use of symbols in understanding the human mind, but took them to represent repressed sexuality or other definitive mental content. For example, anything that is erect or can be erected, or can penetrate, is regarded in Freudian theory as a symbol of the male sex organs, while anything that can be entered or penetrated is a symbol of the female. To use Jung's terminology, Freud saw symbols only as signs – concrete expressions of a known reality. However, to Jung, male and female sexuality were themselves only expressions of deeper creative forces. Even when the intellect tells us that a symbol is manifestly sexual, it is possible to go beyond this interpretation and discover a further breadth of diversity and implication, and a metaphoric and enigmatic portrayal of psychic forces.

The Jungian View

THE ARCHETYPES

The human race has always used symbols to express its awareness of the dynamic, creative forces underlying existence – variously believed to be the elements, the gods or the cosmos. At a more conscious level, symbols, particularly symbolic stories such as myths and legends, have been used to express abstract qualities, such as truth, justice, heroism, mercy, wisdom, courage and love. In Jungian terms, we are all born with instinctive predispositions toward these qualities, a set of internal blueprints of what it means to be fully human. These blueprints, or archetypes, have a dynamic aspect: they can be thought of as bundles of psychic energy that influence the manner in which we understand and react to life, and through which we develop motives, ideals, and certain facets of personality. Although they reside deep within the unconscious, the archetypes can be stimulated

The Archetypes

to emerge into consciousness, where they express themselves in the form of symbols and symbol systems.

According to Jung, we move toward psychological health when we recognize and reconcile our conflicting archetypal energies. This can be achieved through psychotherapy, by the careful study of dream symbolism, or by using symbols themselves as the point of departure. Instead of waiting for the archetypal symbols to emerge from the unconscious, existing symbols can be used as a focus for meditation, and thus provide pathways into the unconscious. The quest for self-knowledge through symbols is not the exclusive territory of Jungian psychology: to know oneself is an aspect of enlightenment in all the great philosophical and religious traditions.

IDENTIFYING THE ARCHETYPES

From his clinical studies and surveys of myth and tradition, Jung identified the main archetypal influences on human

The Archetypes

thought and behaviour. The **anima** is the female archetype, the collective, universal image of woman embedded in the male unconscious. It manifests itself as sentimentality and a tendency toward moodiness, compassion and tenderness. The anima appears symbolically in legends and dreams as the princess imprisoned in a tower or the mysterious enchantress weaving magic spells. In its negative aspect, the anima can appear as the heartless, calculating female who lures a man, only to reject him when he is hopelessly ensnared. The **animus**, the collective image of man in the female unconscious, emerges symbolically as the ideal of manhood – the hero in shining armour, the adventurer who becomes a prince or overcomes evil – or in its negative aspect as the cruel, destructive man who treats a woman as a sex object and discards her once he has robbed her of her virginity and tired of her. It is the

THE ANIMUS
A woman's animus is initially symbolized typically as a physical, athletic man, who evolves into a romantic "man of action" onto whom youthful desires are projected. Later, it often becomes a father-figure or spiritual leader.

side of woman that is aggressive, power-seeking and opinionated.

Powerful processes are also at work with the other archetypes. While the **mother** archetype, the nurturing, caring side of human nature, begins to express itself from birth in a child's suckling and attachment behaviour, the **father** archetype typically emerges later (studies show that a child prefers a woman's voice to a man's in the early months of

THE ANIMA

The anima may appear in myth as goddess, prostitute, fairy or witch. In its negative aspect, it is often personified as a seductress who brings about a man's humiliation or demise. It is here embodied by Salome, who beguiled Herod into promising her anything: she demanded the head of John the Baptist. In its positive aspect the anima is credited with spiritual powers and the hidden wisdom of the Earth, the elements and the oceans.

The Archetypes

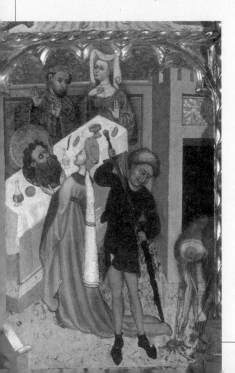

The Archetypes

life). The father is the lord over the material, temporal world, while the mother is the ruler of the unseen world of emotions and feelings. In its positive aspect the father archetype is the protective presence, the wise king of legend, the just lawgiver and judge. In his negative aspect he is the monstrous tyrant, the Greek god Cronos who devours his own children.

The **trickster** archetype is the disruptive, rebellious energy that enjoys denying or questioning the status quo. The trickster has no obvious moral code beyond its urge to disrupt and ridicule. At worst the trickster can destroy our self-confidence and overturn our most cherished beliefs, but it can also serve positive ends, prodding us out of complacency and forcing a re-examination of our goals. In myth, the trickster is best sym-

THE MOTHER
In myth and legend the mother appears in the guise of Nature, the bountiful Earth-mother, as goddesses of fertility, or as nurturing animals such as the cow or she-wolf.

bolized by the Norse god Loki, who variously aided or tricked his fellow gods, depending on whim.

The **shadow** is disruptive energy of a different kind. It is the self-willed, self-seeking part of human nature, which projected outward is the urge to find a scapegoat and to victimize those least able to defend themselves. But it also has a positive role, setting up a creative tension with the sustaining, archetypal aspects within us, giving us something to push against in life, an inner obstacle to overcome. Although the shadow is an essential part of the psyche, we commonly repress it during the early years of life, in the process of socialization, to be more worthy of our parents' love. Accepting the shadow in later life requires considerable moral effort.

The Archetypes

CULTURAL PERSPECTIVES

Cultural Perspectives

THE SHADOW
The shadow
archetype (see
page 23) is an
expression of the
base, antisocial
desires that we
seek to bury in
the unconscious,
which we feel
might impel us
to destructive
acts should we
ever lose our
tight control
over it. In this
16th-century
Indian painting
it is embodied
by the giant
Zammurrad,
who is forced to
remain in a well.

Assuming that the most powerful symbols arise from archetypes – aspects of the collective unconscious – why are their uses and meanings not consistent across cultural boundaries? For example, the genitalia are never used symbolically in Christian art, but in the East they are revered spiritual symbols. In the West, a fat belly is a symbol of gluttony, whereas to the Chinese it is an attribute of the god of wealth and in India it is associated with Ganesha, the elephant god of sacred wisdom. Even colours can carry different symbolic meanings: in Europe yellow connotes deceit and cowardice, but it is the imperial colour in China and in Buddhist tradition it stands for humility and renunciation.

The underlying reason for these differences is that the symbols used to portray archetypal energies are subject to the creative limitations of the human mind. Two individuals looking at the

Cultural Perspectives

same clouds will see in them different shapes. In each case the stimulus is the same, but the response made to it depends upon the observer. At the cultural level, this process of differentiation receives further stimuli from the natural environment. For example, in parts of the arid Middle East sand came to symbolize purity, since it was used for washing in place of water, but in the wetter countries of Europe it became associated with instability and impermanence. The identities of a culture's gods – often the embodiments of Jungian archetypes – were also shaped by environment. The Norse gods displayed the qualities needed to survive in a cold, harsh climate – ferocity, determination, extroversion and intense physicality. However, the Hindu gods, though still representing the same archetypes, are subtler and

THE SCARAB
The symbolism of animals often reflects aspects of their behaviour. In ancient Egypt, the birth of the scarab (dung beetle) from its egg in a ball of dung was seen as an act of self-generation, and it came to represent rebirth, regeneration and renewal.

more spiritualized, reflecting the slower pace of life on the Indian subcontinent.

Human nature thrives upon opposition and difference. Ethnic groups living close to each other often deliberately exaggerated small variations in the attributes of gods and goddesses into major discrepancies, each group claiming a right to an exclusive truth. When one culture or one religion overcame another, it either absorbed the gods of the defeated group, adapting them to fit its own beliefs and iconography, or anathematized them. As Christianity spread across Europe, it largely supplanted the pagan religions through systematically persecuting their adherents. However, when Buddhism arrived in Tibet in the 7th century CE it adopted many symbols and practices from the indigenous shamanistic religion, converting native deities into Buddhist bodhisattvas and lesser divinities.

Finally, symbols often become modified with the passage of time. As

Cultural Perspectives

a culture increases in longevity, there is a tendency to regard the beliefs of previous generations as being primitive or superstitious. Their symbols are rationalized and sanitized, interpreted literally, or simply abandoned altogether by the cultural elite

THE DRAGON
In the West, the dragon symbolizes humankind's basic, primeval nature and the forces of Satan. But the Chinese dragon (above) represents joy, dynamism, fertility and health.

(as has happened with a great deal of religious and mystical symbolism in the scientific West). Stripped from their context, such symbols diminish in power and have to be rediscovered afresh, just as Jung rediscovered the power of archetypal symbols when his patients spontaneously generated them in their dreams, sketches and paintings.

天ノ鈿女命

THE POWER OF SYMBOLS

Symbols tend to accumulate their meanings slowly, over hundreds of years. Like words, their connotations proliferate along many branches, dividing, following a variety of distinctive routes according to cultural context. However, some symbols, or types of symbols, are so universally potent, so close to the very stuff of life, that their meanings tend to remain constant or to vary within a much narrower spectrum.

Unsurprisingly, there is often a connection between the power of symbols and their antiquity. For primitive societies the most basic requirements of life – warmth, food, shelter, sex – loomed large. Alongside the instinct to survive and reproduce was the instinct to find meanings, to make more sense of the necessities on which life depended. For example, we presume that the sun was an object of intense speculation, and certainly in due course it became the theme of some of humankind's most powerful myths. As civilizations developed, these early preoccupations retained their force, and even today the symbols connected with them resonate with significance.

Many of us still believe that profound realities dwell beyond the reach of objective reason. We are ready to acknowledge that such truths are eternal and we sense instinctively that the language of symbolism will give us access to them. This in part explains why even ancient symbols seem full of potential energy, as if addressing some hidden centre within ourselves. Such powerful, far-reaching connotations are the theme of the following section, which traces the development of symbols in religion, myth, ritual, prayer and magic, and looks at some key themes in the language of symbolism.

PALEOLITHIC ART IN THE LASCAUX CAVES

The Lascaux grotto contains probably the finest existing display of prehistoric painting. Hundreds of images cover the walls of the main cave and its connecting galleries: many are high up on the walls and would have required some form of scaffolding. Many of the animal paintings are anatomically accurate and well executed, employing innovative artistic devices to convey perspective.

Symbols in Prehistory

The ability to devise, manipulate and comprehend symbols at an abstract level is one of the main characteristics that distinguishes humans from other primates. Logic, creativity and aesthetics all arise from this ability, which is the cornerstone of the anthropological notion of "culture". The earliest known manifestations of this unique human attribute are the cave paintings of the Paleolithic Period (the Old Stone Age), some of which are more than 30,000 years old.

Paleolithic people were nomadic hunter-gatherers, who were attracted to rock overhangs and cave openings, in which they pitched their skin tents. Archaeological evidence suggests that they did not live in the interiors of caves, which were dark, wet and unstable. The most celebrated Paleolithic paintings are found deep in the cave systems of Lascaux in France and Altamira in Spain, suggesting that this early art was not

Symbols in Prehistory

Symbols in Prehistory

intended to be viewed, and that its function was not merely decorative. Many anthropologists now believe that cave paintings were of profound symbolic significance, and that the cave itself was a sacred place of initiation. The symbols encountered in cave paintings fall into two main categories – naturalistic depictions of animals, and abstract, sometimes geometric, forms. Interpretations of these symbols are highly speculative. Early anthropological studies took the paintings of horses, bison, oxen and mammoth to be a form of sympathetic magic, arising from a belief that the depiction of success in the hunt would be translated into reality. Later explanations, however, held that the spatial arrangements of animal images were of cosmological significance. The abstract symbols, such as quadrangles, spirals

THE POWER OF MASKS

In many societies, to wear a mask was to invoke a supernatural being. In Africa, masks were used to ward off enemies, to summon ancestors, and in rituals and ceremonies that marked tribal alliances.

THE GODS OF EGYPT

In ancient Egypt certain animals were considered to be the manifestations of the gods on earth. The creator sun god, for example, could appear as the Benu bird, a crested grey heron (right) venerated at Heliopolis.

Symbols in Prehistory

THE ELEMENTS

In the ancient world, the destructive power of the elements is a symbol of divine punishment for human failings. Flood myths feature in many cultures, the best known being the biblical story of Noah (left).

35

and groups of dots or lines, show little variation in form over 20,000 years, an extraordinary continuity that is unique in art history. This fact alone suggests that such symbols were of great significance, but their meanings remain unclear. They may have served a calendric or magical function. One recurring motif is a group of seven dots or parallel lines; even to this day the number seven is widely considered to be sacred (see page 105).

Early peoples responded to the natural world at an intuitive level. They may have believed (as did later cultures) that consciousness was shared by all things, animate and inanimate alike, and that this consciousness could be addressed through symbols. From this belief sprang rituals such as rain dances, in which the sound of rain falling on the ground was imitated by the stamping of feet, and fertility dances, which were thought to induce the return of life in the spring. The prominent place of fertility in ancient symbol systems is also apparent from so-called "Venus" sculptures – the small ivory, stone or clay figures of large-breasted women found right across Eurasia.

By the Neolithic Period (the New Stone Age, around 10,000 years ago) people had adopted a more sedentary existence, living in larger communities, and modifying and cultivating the land to suit their requirements. This change in lifestyle prompted the development of more organized public rituals. For example, archaeological evidence (pottery, food and ornaments found in Neolithic funeral mounds) points to the proliferation of funerary symbolism. Death was regarded as a journey, on which the deceased were symbolically accompanied by essential provisions and treasured possessions.

Symbols in Prehistory

TOTEM POLE
For the Native North Americans of the northwest coast, the animals, beings and symbols carved on totem poles were heraldic symbols of tribal or family identity.

GODS AND MYTHS

Gods and Myths

There are no more powerful symbols than the gods. In Jungian terms, the divinities, and the myths that set out their relationship with humankind, are conscious expressions of unconscious, archetypal energies (see pages 18–19). The deities and their associated symbols emerge from, and are given form within, our own psychological lives, but they address the unconscious at such a profound level that they appear to come from some source outside ourselves. They are, according to Jung, embodiments of humankind's "natural religious function", an aspect of the psyche that must be developed to ensure psychic health and stability.

If this explanation sounds as if it reduces the gods – or God – to figments of our collective imagination, this is not so. For it does not

AZTEC GODS
From the 12th to 16th centuries CE the Aztecs built up a powerful empire in what is now Mexico. Aztec religion and myth incorporated elements from the cultures they subdued, and the Aztec pantheon was accordingly large and diverse. In the 260-day ritual calendar, each day was governed by one of 20 deities.

deny that the collective unconscious may be in communication with an even deeper substratum of reality that represents the true creative source of our individual lives. Jungians say that we must recognize that this source, when discovered, can only reveal itself to us in a limited, and limiting, symbolic form.

Although they originate in the human psyche, the gods of most cultures have been externalized, their energies projected on to the outside world, in order to make their presence more immediate and tangible. For example, in ancient Egypt the gods were symbolized by animals that best exemplified their powers. Thus the falcon, soaring high in the heavens and with a sharpness of vision from which nothing can hide, symbolized Horus, lord of the sky.

THE ROLE OF MYTH

Myths are symbolic narratives – tales of divinities, humans with superhuman powers, and extraordinary events – that

Gods and Myths

Gods and Myths

were once of central importance in all cultures. It was through these allegorical tales that a society could establish and explore its identity; and, in many cultures, myths provided a stylized model for human behaviour. The French anthropologist Claude Lévi-Strauss suggested that the purpose of myth was to provide a logical model capable of making sense of the world around them. This interpretation accounts for some components of myth, but it cannot fully explain all the ways in which myth is observed to function in society.

Some myths explain the state of things, such as the origin of maize; others account for the creation of humankind: for example, the Shilluk people of the Sudan, tell how Juok (God) made humans from clay, using black earth to make Africans and white clay to fashion Europeans. The creation stories of many ancient civilizations – from Egypt to China – invoked myths of royal divinity in order to legitimize the social and polit-

Gods and Myths

LORD VISHNU
Vishnu – protector of the world, humanity and *dharma* (moral order) – is one of Hinduism's great deities. In this 17th-century illustration, he takes the form of Matsya, a fish, to warn Manu, the first human, of an imminent deluge.

Gods and Myths

ical order. Myths also address the question of mortality and describe the ultimate fate of the self. The ancient Egyptian *Book of the Dead*, a collection of magical and religious texts, chronicles the passage of the soul through the afterlife in meticulous detail, giving precise instructions on how the departed must meet each of the challenges and opportunities which he or she will face in the underworld.

Freud saw myth as society's way of giving vent to repressed ideas and experiences. For example, he developed the theory of the "Oedipus complex", whereby, he claimed, sons harboured repressed erotic feelings for their mothers and associated feelings of antipathy toward their fathers. Freud claimed that this complex was exposed in the Greek myth of Oedipus, who – unaware of their identities – slew his long-lost father, King Laius, and married his mother, Jocasta. Learning the truth of

GODDESS OF THE DAWN
The movements of celestial bodies were often attributed to divinities. The Greeks personified dawn as the goddess Eos (the Roman Aurora) who emerged every morning from the ocean and rose into the sky on a chariot drawn by a pair of horses.

what he had done, he blinded himself. For Freud, the myth expressed people's collective guilt at harbouring such feelings toward their progenitors.

In Jungian psychology, myths are symbolic journeys through life. Thus, in myths narrating the deeds of heroes, the hero is taken to symbolize the ego, and the stories relate how the hero becomes aware of his strengths and weaknesses (develops his "ego-awareness"). Once he is master of his ego, he dies, usually through an act of self-sacrifice, which symbolizes his passing into maturity. The hero is often guided by an adviser or tutor, who in Jungian terms corresponds to the whole psyche, the complete human identity, which provides the resources that the ego lacks.

Gods and Myths

MA GU

In Chinese myth, Ma Gu (below) was a beneficent sorceress who personified the goodness in all people. In this 2nd-century CE painting, Ma Gu reclaims a large tract of land from the sea to plant it with an orchard of mulberry trees.

RITUAL, MAGIC AND PRAYER

Ritual, Magic and Prayer

Rites and rituals are an important feature of all societies, past and present. They help to maintain the integrity of a community and prepare individuals for the roles they are expected to play within it. Not surprisingly, rituals are most prominent in small, close-knit tribal groups, although they persist in Western societies, where, for example, marriage and funerals are still generally observed.

Rituals are physical enactments of spiritual journeys – or, in Jungian terms, journeys into the collective unconscious – in which the body is the symbol of the

WEIGHING THE HEART
In Egyptian belief, the deceased was ceremonially judged by a panel of deities presided over by Osiris, the lord of the underworld. The heart of the deceased, which was believed to be the seat of truth, was weighed against a feather (left). If the scales balanced, the deceased passed into the blessed afterlife. But if the heart tipped the scales it was judged heavy with sin and was at once devoured by a monster.

spirit. They can sym-
bolize progression to
enlightenment or to
the gods, or the jour-
ney of death and
rebirth, in which we
pass renewed into the
next stage of life. In
many religions, rituals
mirror the supposed
order of the sacred
realm, and thus
establish a closer link
between the human
and divine worlds.
For example, the
Roman Catholic Church observes seven
sacraments – baptism, confirmation,
eucharist, penance, holy orders, matri-
mony and extreme unction (anointing
before death) – which it claims were
instituted by Christ. Numerous religions
have purification rites to remove bodily
pollution, which is thought to be offen-
sive to the gods.

Ritual, Magic and Prayer

EUCHARIST
Christianity's
central rite
involves consum-
ing consecrated
bread and wine
(viewed, literally
or symbolically,
as the body and
blood of Christ).
In this 16th-cen-
tury symbolic
depiction of the
Crucifixion, a
chalice fills with
Christ's blood.

Ritual, Magic and Prayer

In tribal societies, initiation rituals often mark the passage from boyhood into adulthood. They often involve the deliberate infliction of pain (such as circumcision or tattooing), trials of strength and endurance, or a lengthy period of fasting, in order to add a physical dimension to the symbolic invocation of death and rebirth. Similarly, a young girl may pass into maturity through fertility rites involving movement and dance or through symbolic beatings that represented her passivity and submission to the physical demands of womanhood (menstruation, pregnancy and child rearing). These rites of passage involve an irrevocable break with the childhood world, during which, according to Jung, the parental archetypes are damaged (through symbolic death) and the ego is consolidated with the larger group.

Marriage is another type of initiation ritual that may use rings, tattoos and special garments to signify new social status. The ritual itself often involves a

symbolic acting out of the new respon-
sibilities of both partners toward each
other and their families. For the man in
particular, marriage represents a loss of
independence – in Jungian terms, the
sacrifice of the hero archetype – which
in some cultures is offset by the symbolic abduction or rape of the bride. The
idea of sacrifice as a way of bringing
about renewal also lay behind the midwinter fertility rituals carried out in many
cultures to ensure the return of light and
life in the spring.

The belief that nature and the will of
the gods could be influenced by rituals
and symbols was also the fundamental
principle of magic. The magician's aim
was to move progressively through the
planes that were thought to make up
existence, eventually to merge into the
ineffable reality from which, in mortal
life, men and women stand exiled. In
raising himself or herself toward the
gods, the magician had a responsibility
to influence them in beneficial ways. In

Ritual, Magic and Prayer

Ritual, Magic and Prayer

all occult systems, from the Egyptian and Greek mysteries to the Native American tradition and the work of the European alchemists and Kabbalists, the true magician was engaged on a serious quest which had nothing to do with personal power or ill will toward others.

Prayer may be a personal or collective act of communication with the sacred. In either case, it is often surrounded by symbolism and ritual. In most religions, bodily posture and the position of the hands indicate submission and homage. Objects are sometimes used: in Tibetan Buddhism, for example, the mantra written on a prayer flag is believed to be activated by the wind. The Islamic devotional prayer, the *salat*, is governed by ritual. It is performed five times a day, as it was during Muhammad's lifetime, and is preceded by rites of ablution. During the prayer, the faithful face Mecca and perform the *rak'ah*s, the physical postures that accompany recitations from the Koran.

MALE AND FEMALE

Images of man and woman are of deep symbolic significance in their own right. In Jungian psychology they are thought to be conscious expressions of the animus and anima archetypes (see pages 20–21), and in many cultures they appear together as symbols of fertility and the endless renewal of life. Taken separately, at a more esoteric level, man and woman symbolize separation and incompleteness: alone, each is barren and unfruitful, one half of a whole.

The theme of separation reveals itself in numerous myths and legends, from Isis and Osiris, and Orpheus and Eurydice, to Tristram and Iseult, in which man and woman struggle against overwhelming odds to be united. In Egyptian cosmology, heaven and earth (which were believed once to have been united) were represented as man (the earth god

THE CHEMICAL WEDDING
Alchemists believed that their chemical processes could bring nature to perfection (symbolized by the transformation of base metal into gold). A crucial stage was the uniting of the male and female principles of matter – sometimes symbolized as a hermaphrodite (below).

COLOR COELESTINUS.

Male and Female

Male and Female

Geb) and woman (the sky goddess Nut). Even when man and woman come together in the act of love, their union must stop short of a full merging. Thus, many major spiritual and occult traditions have taught that completion can be achieved only internally, in the union of the male and female principles that we each carry within us.

In the East, this idea of inner union finds expression in the Taiji symbol (see pages 53 and 216), and in Hindu and Buddhist Tantra, where male and female deities entwine in an embrace so intricate that the two appear to inhabit one body. Western occult and alchemical traditions embodied the attainment of inner reconciliation (and therefore of true wisdom) as the hermaphrodite (or androgyne), who is at once male and female (see pages 49 and 253). In shamanic religions, the male priest often dresses as a woman to recreate symbolically the state of primordial perfection that existed before the sexes were separated.

Male and Female

KRISHNA AND RADHA
Krishna, a manifestation of Vishnu, is one of the best-loved Hindu gods. With his flute playing he enchanted the *gopi*s (milk-maids) of Brindaban. His favourite was Radha, and their love is a popular subject of art, as shown by this painting from 1780.

OPPOSITION AND UNITY

Opposition and Unity

All the great forces of nature and the human emotions are, in part, defined by their opposites. Without light, there would be no concept of darkness; without sorrow, the experience of joy would be diminished. Just as male and female can be unified at the esoteric level (see page 49), all opposites can be reconciled to recreate the paradisal primordial state. Many Eastern traditions hold that

opposites arose when the one true reality fragmented into apparent disunity to create the world of forms: each fragment is incomplete in itself and longs to be reunited with the original wholeness.

By making sharp distinctions we are blinded to the fact that all opposites in reality spring from the same source, and

TWO REALMS
Many cultures divided the cosmos into heaven and the earthly realm. Heaven is the home of higher powers and earth is the place of matter and physicality.

that the whole of creation is in truth still one. The opposites, and the material world which they constitute, are a subjective reality, and the enlightened mind can see through this to the unity which is its true nature.

The unity underlying diversity, and the mutual interdependence of opposites, is expressed symbolically in numerous objects and shapes. A cup, for example, illustrates that form cannot exist without space, and vice-versa. The sides of the cup belong to the world of form, while the space they contain belongs to the world of emptiness. Form and space together are expressions of the fundamental unity of the cup. Symbols such as the circle illustrate wider aspects of this truth. Although we regard concepts such as "beginning" and "end" as opposites, each point on the circumference of a circle can be both a beginning and an end. Accordingly, the Chinese Taiji symbol (right) is enclosed in a circle, and in Zen Buddhism the

circle stands for enlightenment and the perfection of humanity in unity with the primal principle. In Hinduism and

Buddhism, it is said that "life and death are the same": even the two most fundamental opposites – existence and non-existence – are mutually dependent, and are facets of the same unity.

Opposition and Unity

GOOD AND EVIL ANGELS In this 18th-century print by William Blake, the angels Los (imagination) and Orc (energy and revolt) – symbols of humankind's inner conflicts – struggle for possession of a child, a symbol of the lost innocence of undivided Man.

CROSS-CURRENTS

When different peoples come into contact through trade, conflict or migration, their cultural signifiers – or symbols – rarely remain unchanged. The symbols of one group typically enrich, modify or supplant those of the other, and the resulting changes in artistic expression, myth and tradition bear lasting witness to the meeting of the two cultures. For example, the obvious parallels between the Roman and Greek pantheons are no accident. When they conquered Greece in the 3rd century CE, the Romans borrowed heavily from the richer, more developed mythology of the Greeks, and appended the characteristics of the Greek gods to their own deities. The

PRE-CHRIST-
IAN SYMBOLS
Reverence for
the Virgin Mary
may have origins
in the cults of
popular god-
desses of the
Mediterranean
world. The cres-
cent moon at
Mary's feet in
this 13th-century
painting (right)
was linked with
Isis and Artemis.

FROM EGYPT
TO ROME
The migration of
symbols is exem-
plified by this
1st-century CE
fresco from Pom-
peii, which
shows the Egypt-
ian goddesses
Isis and Neph-
thys flanking a
sacred crocodile.

Cross-currents

Greek Dionysus was incorporated into the Roman Bacchus; and the myths surrounding Artemis, Zeus, Hermes and Aphrodite were projected onto Diana, Jupiter, Mercury and Venus respectively. Apollo was taken over in name as well as in function by the Romans. A similar process of absorption occurred when Buddhism reached Tibet in the 7th century CE (see page 27).

The organized "export" of religion (and therefore of symbols) began in earnest in the 4th century CE, following

Cross-currents

Cross-currents

the adoption of Christianity as the official religion of the Roman empire. With state support, Christianity actively suppressed all forms of paganism. But indigenous beliefs and symbols proved difficult to eradicate, and there was tacit toleration of those symbols that could readily be Christianized, while others were recognized as partial statements of a spiritual reality that reached its final consummation in the coming of Christ. In particular, many stories surrounding legendary early Christian saints seem to be based on pre-Christian myths. Saint Christopher, who is usually depicted as a giant carrying the Christ-child across a river, echoes Charon, who in Greek myth was charged with ferrying the souls of the deceased over the river Styx. Saint Catherine of Alexandria, from whose veins milk was said to have flowed after her martyrdom, carries echoes of the Egyptian goddess Isis, one of whose attributes was milk. Similarly, the attributes of Saint Brigid bear a striking resemblance to those of the Irish goddess of the same name.

SIRENS
Armand Point's *The Siren*, 1897, is typical of a genre in 19th-century art that drew inspiration from the themes in classical mythology.

THE USES OF SYMBOLS

In their infinite variety, symbols have enriched the life of the mind through the centuries. Cultures in all parts of the world have developed and built upon an understanding of symbols and symbol systems to promote spiritual, bodily and intellectual well-being. The following section looks at three very different ways in which the mind or the imagination could be said to employ symbols: art, meditation and dreaming.

Symbolism nourishes artistic endeavour both consciously and unconsciously. In many traditional cultures, much art is purely symbolic in content, expressing in visual terms the beliefs and aspirations of the community. In Western civilization, art began to lose some of its more explicit symbolic purpose with the rise of the notion of artistic individualism – symbolism, after all, is an essentially collective activity. However, there were various ways in which symbolism in art remained current: as an expression of archetypal themes; as a conscious exploitation of traditional imagery; or as a

means of communicating private messages. In modern times, the widespread interest in the intricate workings of the mind has prepared the ground for a tradition of expressly symbolic art – a tradition which has continued to resist the enticements of abstraction.

Meditation reflects a deep-rooted belief, in many cultures, that discipline of the mind, correctly applied, can lead to a form of psychic, spiritual or bodily enhancement, or even to an ultimate reality (often referred to as "enlighten-ment") that would otherwise be inacces-sible. Getting in touch with the inner self, and silencing the myriad distrac-tions that disturb our peace, are dual aspects of this process. In mystical forms of meditation, symbols such as  the wheel or lotus provide access to a higher reality.

Dream symbolism is a vast subject in itself, and in the section that follows we can do little more than generalize. Interpretation of dream symbolism is compli-cated by the need to take into account the individual circumstances and per-sonality of the dreamer. Nevertheless, a knowledge of the Jungian archetypes is extremely helpful, and by recording and questioning our dreams over a period of time we may gain valuable insights into the messages that they bring from the unconscious.

SYMBOLS IN ART

The history of art is a record of humankind's most moving and meaningful symbols. From the Paleolithic Period (see pages 32–34) onward, artists have made use of symbols to express the beliefs and preoccupations of their time. Artefacts of all civilizations bear witness to the intimate relationship between religion and symbolism. In ancient Egypt, stonemasons would inscribe statues of kings and noblemen with the names of their owners in the belief that the statues would provide eternal resting places for their spirits

THE ANNUNCIATION
Renaissance artist Domenico Veneziano uses the symbolism of colour and geometry in his painting of the angel Gabriel's annunciation to Mary that she will conceive a son by the Holy Spirit. The white lily, for example, is a symbol of Mary's purity and humility.

Symbols in Art

after death. Stelae (inscribed slabs of stone) set up at tombs of less mighty individuals had a similar function. Decorated with carvings showing the deceased beside a table laden with offerings to the gods, and inscribed with magical symbols and ritual prayers to Osiris (lord of the underworld), they were designed to ensure the safety of the deceased's soul.

Although funerary and decorative art dating from the Bronze Age (*c.*3000–1100BCE) has been found in northern Europe, the most significant developments in Western art throughout this period took place in the flourishing towns and cities of the Mediterranean. Europe's first civilization, the Minoan culture of Crete, which owed much to the earlier cultures of Egypt and Mesopotamia, made extensive use of spirals, wavy lines and other geometric motifs in its pottery and metalwork. It is believed that these symbols,

EVANGELISTS
Medieval depictions of the authors of the four Christian gospels in symbolic form as man, lion, ox and eagle were inspired by the four creatures in the vision of the prophet Ezekiel.

which echoed the sea and the elements, were expressions of a sense of shared existence with nature. Minoan frescoes often depict rituals, religious ceremonies and battles, and frequently feature bulls, griffins and other animals that may have had a symbolic protective value.

Following the demise of the great Minoan and mainland Mycenaean kingdoms in the 13th century BCE, the geometric style of these earlier cultures were refined and the symbolism of abstract forms – zigzag designs, triangles, meanders and swastikas – dominated Hellenic art for four centuries. It was not until the 8th century BCE that symbolism in Greek art reached new levels of pictorial expression and clarity. At this time, stereotyped animals and human figures, rituals and battles began to appear as themes on ceramics and other artefacts; and narrative art, which chronicled the deeds of gods and heroes, began to emerge by c.700BCE. The figures in these narratives were

Symbols in Art

vivid embodiments of unconscious archetypes. In art, as well as in philosophy and myth, they symbolized the quest for self-knowledge and served as metaphors for all aspects of public and private life. Greek artists borrowed heavily from the cultures of Syria, Phoenicia and Egypt. Mythical creatures from the Near East – Gorgons, Harpies, the Chimera – were Hellenized, becoming more elegant and less frightening. Moreover, Egyptian influence began to stimulate the creation of large, free-standing statues, which evolved in due course into the naturalistic harmony and beauty of Classical Greek sculpture.

A similar emphasis upon the visual power of symbols to alter consciousness is apparent in the art of India and the East. The erotic couplings of the Hindu deities symbolize the diversity of creation, as well as the Tantric techniques which allow sexual union to serve as a path to enlightenment. The *lingam* (symbolic phallus) of Shiva (see page

209) symbolizes not only creative energy but also the number one (primal unity), while other erotic sculptures use sexuality to represent the joys of heaven and eternal bliss. In painting, a common theme is Krishna's amorous adventures with the milkmaids (*gopis*), which symbolize the entry of divine love into the world (see illustration on pages 50–51), or the five universal pleasures embodied in meat, alcohol, grain, fish and sex.

Chinese art has always been exalted in purpose, striving to inspire and educate the viewer, and provide insights into the nature of humankind and the Great Ultimate. Spiritual and moral messages were conveyed through certain "noble" themes, particularly landscapes and the natural world, which developed into highly stylized forms of symbolic expression. For example, every part of the landscape was held to symbolize an aspect of humankind: water was blood, grass and trees were hair, clouds and mists were clothing, and the solitary

Symbols in Art

Symbols in Art

wandering scholar who often featured in such paintings was the soul. Bamboo represented the spirit of the scholar, which could be bent but not broken, and jade stood for purity. Such explicit symbolism was also a feature of architecture. For example, the typical curved gable ends of Chinese buildings were not merely decorative but were believed to launch demons back into space should they try to slide down the roof in an attempt to visit the occupants.

In medieval Europe, representations of Christ, the Virgin Mary and the saints functioned as focal points of worship. Narrative paintings, with their multiple layers of symbolism, served to instruct the illiterate masses in Scripture and the mysteries of the faith, and also to spell out humankind's relationship with God and the cosmos. The artistic devices used to express the essence of the faith emphasized the otherworldliness of God, the great distance between heaven and earth, and the idea that salvation

Symbols in Art

HINDU GODS
Hindu deities
are identifiable
by their distinc-
tive attributes.
Kali, enemy of
demons, is here
a fierce hag
who sits astride
her consort,
white-skinned
Shiva. Brahma,
the creator god
(right), is usu-
ally shown with
four faces.

could be achieved only through the ele-
vation of the spirit. This mystical view of
the universe was reflected in all forms of
art and literature, but perhaps most
spectacularly in the towering Gothic
cathedrals, which were often made to
seem even taller by the skilful manipu-
lation of perspective.

The nature of Christian art and symbolism underwent fundamental change
in the Renaissance. Growing rationalism
and knowledge of the natural world,

Symbols in Art

together with the rediscovery of Classical culture, resulted in a greater naturalism in the visual arts. Nature, the human body and Graeco-Roman myth once again became respectable themes in religious painting and sculpture. For example, in his famous painting of the Last Judgment, Michelangelo cast Christ in the role of Apollo or Hercules rather than portraying him as a crucified saviour. Similarly, in Raphael's Loggia in the Vatican, mythical satyrs, nymphs and other beings mix with the more orthodox symbolism of God as grey-bearded patriarch dividing the waters from the land at the creation.

Even when biblical themes ceased to dominate European art, symbolism continued to play an important role because of its close links with creativity itself. Both symbolism and creativity stem from unconscious processes, and some of the symbolic themes in visual art are not apparent to the artists themselves at the time they create their work.

THE SEARCH FOR
INNER WISDOM

MEDITATION
SYMBOLS
Archetypal symbols such as the rosy cross (left) can be a focus for meditation. Gazing at it steadily, try to avoid judging any thoughts that arise. Let it enter your consciousness as if it is communicating with a rosy cross that is already there. As the inner image grows clearer, with closed eyes feel yourself going deeper into the visualization, as if on a journey into yourself.

Patients in Jungian analysis are encouraged to identify and focus upon symbols that hold special meaning for them. At first these symbols may appear spontaneously in their dreams and doodles, but over time they become personalized, take on deeper levels of meaning, and come to represent aspects of the psyche that had previously remained unexpressed or difficult to put into words. By revealing pathways into the psyche, symbols can help the patient to reconcile the demands of the conscious and unconscious minds and thereby, it is hoped, bring about psychological health and stability.

This use of symbols is not the exclusive province of modern psychiatry. All the great religious traditions have, through meditation, harnessed the power of symbols in the quest for inner peace and spiritual wisdom. The essen-

The Search for Inner Wisdom

MANDALA OF THE *BARDO*
This Tibetan mandala is used for meditation on the *bardo*, the "intermediate state" between death and rebirth. The mandala depicts various powerful deities that can be regarded as personifications of the energies (emotional and physical) that go to make up human life.

tial element in meditation is to prevent the mind from becoming lost in random thoughts by focusing upon a single symbol (which may be auditory, visual or tactile) without trying rationally to reflect on its meaning. The symbol stimulates thoughts and insights, which are simply observed and allowed to pass out of awareness. The aim of meditation is to move beyond linguistic interpretations (though these may have their value when thought about consciously afterward) and uncover a level of intuitive understanding beyond language, which profoundly changes the way we experience the world and ourselves.

In theory, anything from a meaningless scribble to an itch on the nose can act as a focus for meditation, but in practice most meditative traditions use archetypal symbols as their points of departure, because they provide a surer pathway back into the collective unconscious from which they originally emerged. In Native North American and

The Search for Inner Wisdom

The Search for Inner Wisdom

other shamanic traditions, nature provides these symbols, so that the meditator might gaze upon distant mountains, listen to the sound of the wind, or concentrate upon the feel of the earth under their seated body. The Cathars, a 13th-century heretical Christian sect, meditated upon the reflection of a candle flame in water, and a flame is used as a focus in certain forms of yoga. Adepts of the Tibetan practice of *tumo* concentrate upon increasing the sense of heat in the depths of the belly and transmitting it, via subtle energy channels, or *chakras*, through the rest of the body. In certain forms of Hindu and Buddhist meditation, a deity or the Buddha is visualized in great detail, replete with symbolic colours and adornments, and then pictured descending through the crown of the meditator's head and coming to rest in the heart. Like all true symbols, these beings are "real" in that they represent a profound reality beyond mere figments of the meditator's imagination.

DREAM SYMBOLS

Dreams are involuntary products of the psyche. They present us with a bewildering array of images and feelings, familiar and unfamiliar, all of which have something to teach us. The communicative power of dreams has been acknowledged for millennia: the ancients credited dreams with the power of prophecy, and in Egypt the gods were believed to speak through the dreams of the Pharaohs. However, the interpretation of dreams has always been beset with uncertainty, because the messages they carry often emerge in an ambiguous and indistinct symbolic form.

Some dreams function at the non-symbolic level (level 1) and can be taken at face value, representing in an easily identifiable form the experiences and preoccupations of the past day or days – material arising mostly from the preconscious (see page 14). Dreams that function at the mundane symbolic level

Dream Symbols

Dream Symbols

(level 2) go much deeper, using symbols to express material that originates primarily in the personal unconscious (see page 14). Such dreams relate to basic physical preoccupations, such as food, bodily comfort and health, emotions and self-sympathy (the so-called "self-preservation needs"), as well as sexual preoccupations, such as sensuality, orgasm and sexual dominance or submission (the so-called "species preservation needs"). Although these themes could be explored linguistically in a dream, they are often so exciting and alarming that if confronted directly by the mind, the result would be instant waking. By disguising as symbols and metaphors the material it is presenting, the dream may be, as Freud put it, the "guardian of sleep", enabling us to enjoy the physical and psychological benefits that sleep brings. Level 2 dreams are often confusing in both content and presentation, reflecting the muddle that constitutes much of our psychological life.

Dreams that operate at the higher symbolic level (level 3) touch on our desire to find a meaning in life beyond the physical, emotional and sexual, and are said to stem primarily from the collective unconscious (see page 14). Jung referred to them as "great dreams", because they carry a powerful, usually uplifting, emotional charge, and may remain clear in the mind of the dreamer for many years.

In most cases these level 3 dreams contain archetypal images, which are part of the universal symbolic language that anthropologists and psychologists have identified running right across cultures. Typically, they are clearly presented and "stage-managed", as if some director had resolved that we should leave the dream theatre with no confusion in our minds.

Level 3 dreams are thought to operate symbolically because they are associated with a part of the unconscious that evolved before humankind

Dream Symbols

NIGHT
TERRORS
Dream images
clearly inspired
this painting,
Henry Fuseli's
The Nightmare.
But even fright-
ening dreams
are trying to
help us. Using
images with suf-
ficient emo-
tional charge to
alert us to their
importance,
they draw our
attention to
aspects of our
psychological
life that we may
be misusing or
neglecting.

acquired speech, and which therefore
functions pre-linguistically. They contain
psychological material that cannot be
put into words; and although the archetypal images they contain may speak
during the dream, their words are associated more with those areas of consciousness which remain active during
sleep than with anything directly
expressed by the symbols themselves. It
is as if the meaning contained in the
symbols is recognized and to some
degree translated into words by the
mind, even during sleep.

Dreams have a quirky, idiosyncratic
way of handling their material. In
dreams, symbols often undergo sudden,
puzzling transformations. We leap onto
the back of a horse only to find it has
changed into a hammock swinging
under a tree. We enter a cave only to
discover ourselves in the nave of a great
cathedral. We open a book that transforms itself into a chessboard complete
with chessmen – and so on. Yet these

Dream Symbols

Dream Symbols

apparently bizarre transformations are accepted without question by the dreaming mind. Either our critical faculties are left behind as we enter through the gates of sleep, or we recognize at the time that these transformations make their own kind of sense.

If they do, what kind of sense might this be? The answer is that symbols and dream events are connected together by meaning rather than by appearance. Thus, the horse changing into a hammock under a tree may indicate that by training an aspect of our powerful, instinctive nature (the horse) we may make life not only easier for ourselves (the hammock) but also more creative (the tree). The position of the hammock, midway between the roots and the branches of the tree, may also suggest a desirable balance between our animalistic side (the earth) and our spiritual side (the crown of the tree). Similarly, the cave changing into the nave of a cathedral may represent the need to go more deeply into the unconscious self (the cave) in order to find not only the space for which we may be longing in life (the vastness of the nave) but also the spiritual direction and guidance (the cathedral itself). And the book changing into a chessboard may show that we need to put our theoretical wisdom (the book) into practice (the chessboard).

We may dream of a train waiting at a crossing which suddenly becomes an elephant charging toward us, and of a gun which we draw to defend ourselves only to see it turn into an empty bottle. This dream seems to be offering us a new opening in our life (the waiting train) provided that we are prepared to change course (the crossing, at which road meets rail). At this point, anxiety enters the dream. The charging elephant (a symbol of higher authority) threatens to crush us unless we defend ourselves. However, our weapon (the gun), turns out to be useless (the transformation into the empty bottle).

Dream Symbols

Dream Symbols

These examples show the clarity with which the dream narrative can be allowed to emerge, provided that we are prepared to spend time consciously analyzing our dream symbols. And just as experience improves our proficiency at spoken languages, so it allows us to become more and more familiar with dream language, and with the way in which, through this language, our unconscious psychological life allows its hopes, warnings and fears to emerge into conscious awareness.

THE WORLD OF SYMBOLS

 Symbols have been subjected to analysis by historians, archaeologists, ethnographers and psychologists. To date, however, no unified theory has emerged to account for the language of symbolism in the same way that grammatical theory explains the fundamental framework of spoken and written language. Symbols, unlike written words, are not limited by practical concerns: their abundance and variety is constrained only by the limits of the human imagination. They appear in every conceivable form – in pictures, metaphors, sounds, gestures, odours, myths and personifications – and draw on all sources, material and non-material, for their inspiration.

Jung argued that symbols constitute a universal idiom. Abstract shapes, which arise directly from the unconscious without any allusion to the natural world, are indeed encountered worldwide. The cross is, of course, best known as a Christian symbol. However,

a cross was used by the Assyrians to represent their sky god, Anu, and by the Chinese as a symbol of the earth. When the Spanish, led by Hernán Cortés, landed in Mexico in 1519, they found in the native temples numerous depictions of the cross – the Toltec symbol of the gods Tlaloc and Quetzalcoatl. The invaders, however, had no conception that the cross could be anything other than a Christian symbol, and concluded that it must have been carried to the Toltecs on one of the missions of Christ's disciple Saint Thomas, whom Christian tradition revered as the apostle of the Indies. This story underlines the point that although symbols are a characteristic feature of humanity in general, they are also subject to widespread differentiation across cultural divides. Cultures and religions are largely defined by the symbols they use and venerate, and initiation into a particular symbol system helps to shape an individual's identity. By denying that the cross could be a Toltec symbol, the Spanish were in effect protecting the integrity of their own religious beliefs.

But symbols are more than just historical and cultural signposts. They can help us toward a fuller understanding of our own minds. The entries on the following pages explore the meanings, esoteric and exoteric, of symbols: representing a sample of the huge array of symbolic forms, they provide an entry into this fascinating world.

SHAPES AND COLOURS

Shapes and colours are the building-blocks of all visual symbols, but are also deeply significant in their own right. Religions such as Judaism and Islam, which have generally forbidden the direct depiction of God, have developed an array of abstract shapes to represent aspects of divine energy. However, symbolic shapes also occur frequently in the cultures of ancient Egypt and Greece, and in those of northern Europe, where naturalistic religious art is highly developed, and abstract symbols, such as quadrangles, circles and rows of dots, were a common theme in art as early as the Paleolithic Period (see pages 32–34).

RAINBOW
In Christianity the colours of the rainbow symbolize the gifts of the Holy Spirit to the Church: sacraments, doctrine, office, polity, prayer and powers to loosen and to bind.

The ubiquity of symbolic shapes stems partly from the fact that they are easily repro-

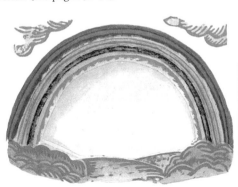

Shapes and Colours

87

Shapes and Colours

duced and recognized, but also suggests that they carry levels of meaning not easily conveyed through representational images. Over the years, simple forms were embellished and elaborated, taking on new nuances of meaning. For example, the Anglican Church, recognizes as authentic at least fifty variants of the Christian cross.

The symbolic language of colour is most easily decoded in relation to the hues of the natural world. For example, the Chinese Han emperors (206BCE–200CE) chose the colour of their ritual robes according to the particular aspect of nature to which their

prayers were addressed. Similarly, Christian priests wear different colours according to the occasion and time of year.

Shapes can be combined to generate new levels of meaning. For example, upward- and downward-pointing triangles (symbols of male and female energies respectively) form a symbol of sexual union when placed point to point.

Shapes and Colours

CONCENTRIC CIRCLES

A series of circles, one inside the other, is widely found as a symbol of the cosmos, as in this 16th-century symbolic map of the universe.

SACRED GEOMETRY

Sacred Geometry

Certain geometrical shapes have the power to reach deep into the unconscious and effect subtle changes in the mood of the observer. This property is perhaps most apparent when applied by a skilful architect. For example, visitors to Classical Greek sites such as the Parthenon often experience a sense of inner tranquillity that can linger for long after. Similarly, the soaring grandeur of Europe's great Gothic cathedrals evokes in the viewer a sense of boundless spiritual possibilities.

The most direct explanation for the psychological power of abstract shapes is that they symbolize certain human emotions. An abrupt shape with irregular, jagged edges for most people symbolizes anger or anxiety, while a symmetrical, rounded shape represents feelings of relaxation and inner peace. It is possible that the near-universal meanings of certain shapes reflect some pat-

CIRCLE

Lacking beginning or end, it represents infinity, perfection and eternity. It is often a symbol of God, and is the form of the halo.

SQUARE

This represents solidity: a perfection that is static, dependable, earthly and material. In Hinduism it stands for cosmic order and the balance of opposites.

tern-making ability within the mind itself. There is evidence that some geometric forms are innately more pleasing than others: certainly, babies are more strongly attracted to symmetrical shapes than to unbalanced, uneven ones.

This preference may have as its source the symmetry of the human face, and the feelings of well-being and comfort associated with the parental face from an early age. Our feelings about geometry may also be concerned with the intrinsic balance within nature itself, each state of mind counterweighted and in part defined by its opposite.

Sacred Geometry

TRIANGLE

Pointing upward, the triangle stands for ascent to heaven, fire, the male principle; downward, grace, descent from heaven, water, the female element.

CRESCENT

The shape of the changing moon, a crescent symbolizes change within the world of forms. An emblem of Islam, paired with a star it represents divinity.

upper circle (1) is
God and the
lower circle (2)
represents the
world of angels
and higher spiri-
tual elements

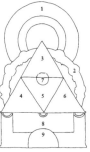

operating under
God. The four tri-
angles represent
heaven (3) rising
above the ele-
ments of earth
(4), air (5) and
water (6).
Humankind is
symbolized by
the circle (7)
straddling heaven
and earth. The

THREE REALMS
This 17th-century
design represents
the realms of
God, Humankind
and Satan. The

rectangle (8) at
the base stands
for hell. Satan is
the semicircle (9),
a symbol of
incompleteness.

WHEEL OF LIFE
The circle as a symbol of the constant cycle of change is used graphically in the Tibetan Buddhist Wheel of Life. At the top are the heavenly realms, followed (clockwise) by the realms of jealous gods, hungry ghosts, animals, and humankind. Holding the wheel is Yama, lord of death, who devours all.

Sacred Geometry

Sacred Geometry

THE OVAL

A symbol of the female genitalia, and thus of the female principle, when horizontal it becomes the all-seeing eye, best known in the form of the Eye of Horus, the Egyptian lord of the skies.

THE SWASTIKA

An ancient symbol long revered in India, it is essentially a spinning cross, the angles at the end of each arm representing light streaming as the cross turns. Spinning anti-clockwise, it represents female energy; clockwise, male.

THE CELTIC CROSS

Pre-dating Christianity, it was originally linked with fertility, the cross symbolizing male generative power and the circle female. As a Christian symbol it stands for heaven and earth in union.

THE INVERTED CROSS

In legend, Saint Peter was crucified upside-down, feeling unworthy to be crucified on the upright cross of Christ. The inverted cross therefore came to represent humility.

THE ANKH

Egyptian gods are often shown holding an ankh, which means "life" and symbolizes immortality. The Coptic church adopted it as its unique form of the Christian cross.

THE ROSY CROSS

Linked with generative power, it was used esoterically by Rosicrucians to suggest Christ's blood spilled on the cross and the seven stages of initiation (the seven rows of seven petals that form the flower).

95

Sacred Geometry

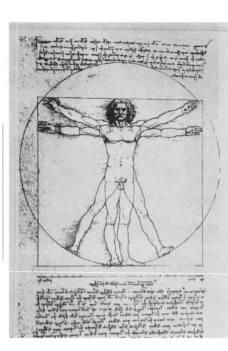

COSMIC MAN

Deities are mostly shown in human form, and in the Bible God made Man "in his own image". The body is held to be a microcosm, a replica of the structure of the cosmos.

EYE

This illustration from an 18th-century Arabic manuscript, shows the eye as an oval containing two circles, the inner of which encloses a mandala of divine wisdom.

Sacred Geometry

SEAL OF SOLOMON
Of great antiquity, the Seal of Solomon has strong associations with Hebrew mysticism. The upward-pointing triangle meets the downward-pointing triangle, the two merging in perfect harmony. The Seal represents the sacred number seven – represented by the six points plus the invisible seventh element of transformation.

STUPA
Built to house sacred Buddhist relics, it is an all-embracing symbol. Its square base represents earth, the circle water, the triangle fire, the semi-circle air, and the flame ether.

PENTAGRAM
The endless five-pointed pentagram stands for perfection and wholeness, the four elements plus spirituality. These properties give the symbol power over evil spirits, and make it a favourite of magicians.

97

Sacred Geometry

CELTIC TRIPLE ENCLOSURE

This represents human consciousness. The outer square is the part of the mind that relates to the physical world. The inner one is the unconscious: through it come visions of gods and other worlds. The middle square represents transition.

PYRAMID

The pyramid's apex symbolizes the highest point of spiritual attainment. Egypt's pyramids were built as pathways for the dead king to rise to the heavens, and as representations of the primeval mound on which creation took place.

MANDALAS AND YANTRAS

In mandalas and yantras, which reach their most intricate and evocative form in the iconography of India and Tibet, the symbolism of geometrical shapes is used to maximum effect. These complex sacred diagrams act as a focus for meditation. They are essentially depictions of the universe and of the forces and gods that drive it. By meditating on the symbol and moving mentally toward its centre, the seeker is made aware of deep levels of meaning.

The shapes that appear most frequently in mandalas and yantras are circles, squares and triangles. Combinations of these forms can produce extraordinary visual effects, conveying the idea that nothing exists except as an encounter between various fields of energy, just as a rainbow is created only when sunlight, water and the

OM MANI PADME HUM The popular Sanskrit mantra *Om mani padme hum* ("*Om* the jewel in the lotus *Hum*") is here represented in mandala-like form. The mantra is in Tibetan script, written in the six lotus petals.

Mandalas and Yantras

99

observer's power of sight come together. Through meditation on the mandala or yantra, the mind is gradually able to "unscramble" the sets of relationships which give an illusory sense of permanence to the outside world. There are no strict differences between mandalas and yantras, but mandalas usually contain script or the human form (Buddhas, bodhisattvas, deities, spiritual masters), while yantras are primarily geometrical. Yantras represent the realities that lie beyond the world of physical forms.

Mandala-like shapes drawn spontaneously by people in psychotherapy with no grounding in Eastern mysticism are thought to represent an attempt by the conscious self to recognize and integrate unconscious knowledge.

SRI YANTRA
Increasingly complex from the centre, this yantra helps us to focus on the moment of creation, both of the cosmos and of thoughts and perceptions.

Mandalas and Yantras

LORD OF
COMPASSION
A Nepalese man-
dala of Avaloki-
teshvara, bodhi-
sattva of compas-
sion, who is
incarnated in the
Dalai Lama. We
can awaken our
own compassion
by meditating on
his mandala.

MAZES AND LABYRINTHS

The maze or labyrinth is of universal fascination. It appears in the symbolism of ancient Egypt and early Mediterranean civilizations. It was depicted by the pre-Christian Celts before appearing as a motif in medieval Christianity, and is also found in Indian and Tibetan cultures. The symbolism of the maze in many of these cultures reflects the idea of an inner journey through the confusing and conflicting pathways of the mind until the seeker reaches the centre and discovers the essential reality of his or her own nature.

Mazes can be formed from hedges, banks or walls, or they can simply be

MINOTAUR
The original Labyrinth was a mythical multicursal maze on Crete which Theseus entered to kill the Minotaur, representing our deepest animal nature.

Mazes and Labyrinths

WAY OF TRUTH
In medieval
Europe the maze
denoted the true
way of Christ.
These two mazes
are from the floor
of Chartres cathe-
dral (above) and
a ceiling in the
ducal palace in
Mantua, Italy.

CLOCK MAZE
Running inex-
orably forward,
the passage of
time is aptly sym-
bolized by the
unicursal maze
in the form of a
clock (left).

traced out on the ground. Not all are
puzzles: "unicursal" labyrinths have a
single winding route to the centre and
there is no fear of losing the way. In
early European civilizations such mazes
were perhaps the scenes of rituals in
which all members of a community
passed through the maze in a symbolic
act of communal togetherness.

In contrast, a "multicursal" maze –
with many blind turnings to disorientate
the seeker – is a much more individual
and potentially threatening exercise. It
symbolizes the way in which the mind
can easily become confused and side-
tracked in its attempts to find the way
back to the source of its being.

Mazes and Labyrinths

DREAM MAZE
Mazes are com-
mon in dreams,
appearing as
bewildering
paths through a
forest or strange
town. They may
represent confu-
sion or indeci-
sion in our life.

NUMBERS AND SOUNDS

Numbers and Sounds

Numbers are far more than a convenient way of measuring the physical world. In many traditions they are considered to be the primal organizing principle that gives structure to the universe. The lives of animals and plants, the seasons and the movements of the planets are all governed by numerical relationships; and the shapes of crystals and harmony in music are determined by numerical laws. Numbers are seen as universal templates of creation, and therefore as symbols of perfection and of the gods. Each letter of the Greek and Hebrew

THREE
The number three underlies all aspects of creation: birth, life, death; past, present, future; mind, body, spirit. Triads occur in many religions, symbolizing unity in diversity. The gifts of the three Magi (below) symbolize Christ's majesty (gold), divinity (incense), and sacrifice (myrrh).

FOUR
The number of four-limbed humankind, completion and wholeness: four elements, cardinal points and seasons. In China it was the number of the earth.

SEVEN
The sum of divinity (three) and humankind (four), seven expresses the relationship between God and the world: seven days of creation, seven deadly sins and seven heavens.

alphabets was assigned a number (a system called gematria) and great importance was attached to the numerical significance of a name or phrase – most famously, "Emperor Nero" in Greek bore the number 666. The idea that all things can be expressed in terms of numbers persists today in numerology.

Sound is an evocative and thus a creative experience. Many cultures

Numbers and Sounds

Numbers and Sounds

credit the gods with the power to make sounds, either through natural agencies, such as wind, water and animals, or through musical instruments. Sound can be bewitching (the song of the Sirens), or destructive (the shout with which the Israelites felled the walls of Jericho). In many mythologies creation begins with a sound disturbing a primordial silence.

OM SRI KRISHNAYA NAMAH

THE MANTRA

In Hinduism and Buddhism the mantra is a sacred sound, which symbolically expresses a particular divine energy. Mantras can be spoken aloud or just sounded in the mind. Initiation into certain sects involves the guru whispering the mantra into the ear of the initiate.

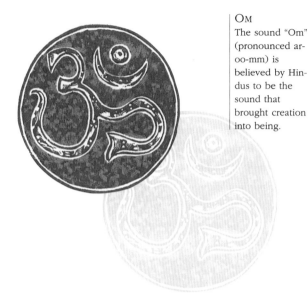

OM

The sound "Om" (pronounced ar-oo-mm) is believed by Hindus to be the sound that brought creation into being.

Numbers and Sounds

M

The letter "M" indicates the union between man and woman, who are shown sheltering under its arches.

COLOURS

Colour is one of the areas in daily life in which symbolism is most readily apparent. This is because colours have an immediate impact on our emotions, possessing the power to arouse or to tranquillize, to gladden or to depress. Psychologists suggest that the effects of colours on the mind derive from their associations with the natural world (blue sky, red blood, gold sun and so on), while occultists put forward more esoteric explanations, linking the seven colours of the spectrum with the magical number seven and with the number of notes on the musical scale.

At a deeper level, colour symbolizes all the aspects and energies of life itself, so that death is seen as either black (the total absence of colour), as in the West, or white (the totality of colour, symbolizing the completion of life), as in the East.

RED
The colour of blood and symbol of the life-force, anger and war. It is the symbol of Christ's passion and of the most vigorously male Roman gods, Jupiter (below) and Mars.

Colours

BLUE

Symbol of intellect, peace and contemplation, of water, sky, infinity and primordial emptiness. The hue of the Virgin Mary as Queen of Heaven (left).

YELLOW

Hinting at some of the qualities of gold, yellow also suggests betrayal and cowardice. In China it was the sacred colour of the emperor (right) and to Buddhists it denotes humility.

VIOLET

The most mystical shade, joining red's power to blue's sanctity. A focus for meditation, it also denotes sorrow. Here, the nymph Echo pines for the love of Narcissus.

Colours

BLACK
Often the hue of death and grief. An approaching black cat is a traditional ill omen. In Egypt black signified rebirth and fertility.

GOLD
A symbol of the sun, divinity and majesty. For the Greeks it denoted immortality, represented by the mythical Golden Fleece (right).

GREEN
The ambivalent colour of growth and decay. A positive link is with Tir Nan Og, the isle of eternal youth of Irish myth (below).

WHITE
Symbol of purity, virginity and, in the East, mourning. It is the hue of Mount Meru, a Tibetan symbol of enlightenment.

OBJECTS

As fragments of the physical world, objects are often imbued with special significance because they span the divide between the inexpressible inner reality that each individual builds up from instinct, intuition and experience, and the outer world of forms. The deepest symbolic meanings are held by objects that resonate with the preoccupations of people everywhere at all times – food, sex, conflict and the gods.

The earliest known sculptures, the "Venus" statuettes of the Paleolithic Period (see page 37), were probably fertility amulets. By handling them (many are polished and worn from touching), perhaps the ancients silently petitioned the spirits believed to rule over birth and regeneration. Such talismans appear in nearly all cultures, and in the West they still survive, albeit in a debased form, as lucky charms. Talismans are usually representations of a god or goddess: they

HOURGLASS
A symbol of mortality and the passing of time, the hourglass also stands for the cyclical nature of existence (because hourglasses have to be inverted repeatedly). It also denotes the grace of the heavens falling upon the earth.

Objects

serve as constant reminders to the deity of the supplicant's existence, but are also embodiments of the god's powers and are themselves capable of influencing events. Other objects help to focus prayer and meditation. The spinning of a Buddhist prayer wheel is a way of offering up a prayer or mantra inscribed upon it or contained within. Similarly, the Christian rosary presents the devotee with a structure for prayer.

When fashioning an object from wood, stone or metal, the artisan is cast in the role of creator. In the belief that an artefact contains its creator's energy, artisans of past civilizations may have engaged in meditation and purification rites before starting work. In Japan this is still the practice among the blacksmiths who make ceremonial weapons.

HOLY GRAIL
The legendary chalice used by Christ at the Last Supper, and later a receptacle for his blood, represents the goal of the spiritual quest, salvation.

ROYALTY, OFFICE AND CONSECRATION

Royalty, Office and Consecration

Many trappings of office are highly expressive symbols of status, helping to maintain the mystique of those in high positions, and setting them apart. Such objects may represent wealth and riches, superior wisdom, access to secret powers, or simply of temporal or spiritual authority. A symbol of office may be an everyday object used as a potent metaphor. Thus the regalia of Egyptian pharaohs and Christian bishops includes a stylized shepherd's crook denoting leadership and protection of "the flock".

FONT
Fonts symbolize entry into the Christian way of life by the sacrament of baptism, a cleansing of sins and symbolic rebirth in the life-sustaining fluid of the earth-mother. Fonts are often eight-sided (the number of regeneration) and placed inside the west entrance to a church.

THRONE

A powerful symbol of dominion, divinity and wisdom, a throne can represent the relationship between God and humanity. An empty throne can symbolizes the Most High, whose features are too glorious to be portrayed.

Royalty, Office and Consecration

115

BASIS VIR·   TVT· VAI CON·   ·STANTIA

COAT OF ARMS

From its origin as
an identification
aid in war, the
coat of arms
became a com-
plex symbol of
identity and sta-
tus. The shield is
the oldest and
most important
element; the crest
and "supporters"
(often animals)
were added later.

OIL LAMP

This lamp bears a
cross, symboliz-
ing Christ as Mes-
siah ("Anointed
One") and Light
of the World.
Anointing with
oil is symbolic of
consecration.

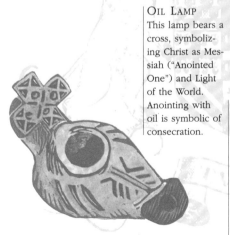

CROWN

As a circle, a crown represents perfection and the infinite; its height denotes majesty. A golden crown symbolizes solar male power; a silver one lunar feminine power.

Royalty, Office and Consecration

ORB

The royal orb (from the Latin *orbis,* "world") surmounted by a cross denotes the dominion of Christ over the world and symbolizes the divine authority that is vested in a Christian monarch.

FLEUR-DE-LYS

The emblem of the kings of France, the thee-petalled fleur-de-lys ("lily flower") stands for the Holy Trinity and the triple majesty of God, creation, and royalty.

WAR AND PEACE

War and Peace

The importance of war and peace in human affairs is reflected in a rich symbolic vocabulary. War is conventionally portrayed as destruction and disturbance of equilibrium, as a violator of beauty or as a visitation of hell upon earth. Peace is seen as healing and fertility, the ravaged land returned to the plough and the weapons of war converted to constructive purposes. However, these depictions are by no means universal. For example, war may be presented as a crusade, a cleansing process or the victory of good over evil, and peace is sometimes represented as sloth, complacency, or the degeneration of youthful vigour. At a psychological level, war can suggest mental turmoil and the battle between the desires of the flesh and the dictates of the spirit. It also represents the destructive forces of madness and

DOVE AND OLIVE BRANCH A symbol of the end of the great Flood, when the dove brought an olive branch to Noah. The dove is a classic symbol of peace, and of the Holy Spirit.

psychological fragmentation. Through its identification with aggressive energy, war can also symbolize masculinity (the deities of war in all cultures are predominantly male) and initiation into manhood. Peace can stand for maturity of mind, and the reconciliation of opposites: associated with passive, receptive energy, it sometimes denotes femininity, the power that creates and nurtures life.

Weapons were often adorned with symbolic forms in the belief that their power would be enhanced. For example, in Christendom the hilt of the sword was often in the form of the cross.

War and Peace

MARS, ROMAN GOD OF WAR
Mars is pictured in a chariot, itself a symbol of battle. The month of March – when armies were mobilized after the winter – is named after him.

APOCALYPSE

The Four Horse-
men are perhaps
the best-known
representations of
the Apocalypse
(the Revelation
of St John in the
New Testament,
which presents
a vision of the
end of the
world). Dürer's
15th-century
engraving *Death,
Famine, War
and Plague: The
Apocalypse* (left)
shows Death
holding
a trident and rid-
ing a sickly,
emaciated horse;
Famine with a
pair of scales;
War carrying a
sword and
accompanied by
an angel; and
Plague wielding
a bow and arrow.

War and Peace

WEAPONS

Like war itself,
weapons can
bear positive
symbolism. The
sword often
stands for justice
and authority;
the bow and
arrow for sunlight
and the pangs of
love; and the
dagger for the
phallus as well
as masculinity
in general.

MUSICAL INSTRUMENTS

Musical Instruments

Music and chant evoke profound states of consciousness and can stimulate mystical experiences. Music symbolized the order and harmony behind creation, and it has seemed natural in most cultures to use music to invoke the divine. In Hinduism, the goddess Lakshmi is believed to reside in musical instruments.

LYRE
The lyre of Orpheus charmed the birds from the trees. Also a symbol of Apollo, god of prophecy, music and light, the lyre represents wisdom and moderation.

DRUM AND DANCE

Rhythm and dance are widely believed to imitate the process of divine creation and to bring us closer to our instinctive natures.

HARP

The Daghda, Irish father god, used a harp to summon the seasons. It also symbolizes the passage to the next world.

HORN

The sounding of a horn heralds the end of the world or, in Jewish tradition, the approach of an enemy.

KNOTS, CORDS AND RINGS

Symbolizing a binding together, knots, cords and rings can have negative connotations or positive ones of unity and initiation. The sacred cord worn by the Hindu Brahmin stands for the link with the absolute. Knots can stand for the tortuous path to enlightenment, while a ring suggests protection and eternity.

Knots, Cords and Rings

THREAD OF LIFE
In Greek myth, the three Fates – Clotho, Lachesis and Atropos – respectively spin, measure and cut the thread of life, apportioning every person's lifespan at the moment of birth.

Knots, Cords and Rings

PLAIT

Featured in Christian architecture, a plait denoted the bond between man and God.

THE SPIRAL

The ancients believed that energy flowed in spiral form. The spiral represents both male and female energies.

ENDLESS KNOT

In Celtic, Hindu, Buddhist and Chinese art, the endless knot (right) features as a symbol of eternity, continuity and longevity.

SILKEN CORD

In occult traditions, the etheric (spiritual energy) body is said to be joined to the physical by means of a silken cord (below).

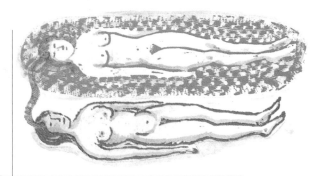

BUILDINGS AND MONUMENTS

From Neolithic times, architecture has served humankind's emotional and spiritual as well as practical needs. Buildings chronicle our developing thoughts about ourselves and the world, and reflect our higher aspirations.

The dimensions of many structures, particularly sacred ones, have been strongly influenced by the symbolic meanings of form. Their architects believed that following certain geometric guidelines would infuse their works with sacred power. For example, Christian churches are traditionally constructed in the form of the cross, and the nave, where the worshippers congregate, symbolizes a ship (Latin *navis*) bearing souls to Christ. The

Buildings and Monuments

CASTLE

Representing the bastion of good or evil, it may be a place where a maiden (often a symbol of enlightenment) is held captive, or treasure is guarded.

towers of Hindu temples represent the cosmic mountains where the gods dwell, and the great Buddhist temple of Borobudur in Java is in the form of a massive mandala – a representation of the cosmos in three dimensions.

Buildings and Monuments

TOMB

The ancients saw the tomb as a gateway to a new life, in which the dead would exist in the same form but in a different dimension.

STONE CIRCLE

These great megalithic structures may have been ritual sites. Some are skilfully aligned with celestial events.

TEMPLE

A sanctuary where the spirit of a deity resided on earth, and a symbol of our striving for nearness to divinity.

Buildings and Monuments

BRIDGE
A common symbol of transition, especially from life to death.

DOOR
A barrier through which only initiates – those with the key – are able to pass.

WINDOW
A symbol of the way in which our consciousness views and interprets the world. A window also represents any means of perceiving God's light.

ANIMALS

The ancient Egyptians believed that certain animals embodied the great divine forces that create and sustain life. In having access to the gods, humankind's position was higher than that of the animals, though this made us vulnerable to confusion and inner conflict. Only by looking to the animal world could we learn how best to develop or curb the creative forces within ourselves.

Similar ideas occur in the shamanic traditions that still find living expression in many parts of the world. Animals are seen as a source of wisdom and power, not because they are greater than humankind, but because they are privy to the secrets of nature in a way that humanity, hampered by intellect, is not. Thus, animals can serve as guides to other worlds, as prophets, and as initiators into secret wisdom. To the shaman, the ability to communicate with animals

MOUSE

Mice symbolize destruction from their gnawing habits; humility from their size.

ANIMAL
SYMBOLS
The profusion of
animal symbolism
in mythology, art
and religion

worldwide is an
acknowledgment
of how power-
fully instinct and
emotion affect
our behaviour.

and the wearing of animal skins symbolize the restoration of the paradisal state.

Even in modern societies, certain animals are held to be omens of good or bad fortune, and some traditions maintain that we should inform animals of important events such as births or marriages. Gods are represented as animals in Hindu art, and in Christian iconography Christ and the Evangelists may appear in animal form (see page 64).

However, it is now more usual for animals to symbolize the baser sides of human nature, such as lust, violence and greed, which must be tamed or killed. Thus Satan may be shown with the horns, hooves and tail of a goat, and in the Tibetan Wheel of Life (see page 93) the cock, snake and pig exemplify those baser human instincts that keep us tied to the realms of birth and death and prevent us from stepping off the wheel into Nirvana.

Animals

BUTTERFLY
Butterflies stand for transformation, immortality, and beauty arising out of apparent death (the seemingly lifeless cocoon).

DRAGONFLY
Symbolising summer in China, the dragonfly also represented instability because of its apparently haphazard flight.

DRAGONS AND SERPENTS

Dragons and Serpents

Dwelling in darkness under the earth, with lungs of fire, the wings of a bird and the scales of a fish, the dragon unites the four elements of the ancient world into a single presence that inspires the imagination and haunts our dreams. In itself neither good nor bad, it symbolizes the primal energy of matter, which can be turned to either good or evil.

In the Far East, the dragon has traditionally represented the positive aspects of this energy. Uniting earth (the serpent) with air (the bird, the breath of life), it represents the coming together of matter and spirit. This beneficent force is thought to animate the earth through

DRAGON RISING FROM THE SEA
In the East, this was linked with scholarship and the creative mind. In the West, it was the symbol of the depths of the unconscious and the strange energies that dwell there.

"dragon pathways" – symbolic arteries through which earth energy flows.

The pre-Christian West also emphasized the positive aspects of dragon energy. But in Christianity the serpent and dragon represent Satan the tempter and stand for chaos, raw destructive power and the evil inherent in the material world. The dragon also came to symbolize the inner world of the emotions and the unconscious. It is the animal energy that lurks within us, which, unbridled, can reduce us to beasts.

DRAGON-SLAYER
This image symbolizes the triumph of spirit over matter. The lance is a symbol of masculine power, and of the sun's rays slanting into the world.

Dragons and Serpents

CHINESE DRAGON

The four claws of Mang, the terrestrial dragon, represent the four elements. Long, the imperial dragon (above), was blessed with a fifth claw, representing ether – the spiritual power that was fully manifested in the person of the emperor.

Dragons and Serpents

SERPENT WITH
SEVEN HEADS
On one level a
symbol of the
Seven Deadly
Sins, this also
combines the
serpent or dra-
gon with seven,
the mystical
number of the
universe, and
as such repre-
sents positive
creative force.

135

Dragons and Serpents

ENTWINED SNAKES

A symbol of the creative interdependence of good and evil. Entwined around a staff, the two snakes form the caduceus, the wand of Hermes (Mercury), the god of transition. It came to be used as a symbol for healing.

OUROBOROS

Found both in ancient Greece and Egypt, the image of a snake swallowing its own tail brings together the symbolism of the circle and the serpent. It represents totality, rebirth, immortality, and the round of existence.

MEDUSA

Medusa made love in a temple of Athene and the outraged goddess changed her into a hag with snakes for hair, whose gaze could turn a man to stone. She symbolizes fear, especially men's fear of women's swift transformations of mood.

HERALDIC BEASTS

Heraldry evolved in medieval Europe as a way to formalize the various emblems adopted by noble families to proclaim their identity and status in a largely pre-literate society. Some families used geometrical designs, but many favoured animals which perhaps echoed the family name or represented qualities that they felt themselves to possess. Some heraldic animals were mythical while others, though based on exotic animals such as lions, leopards and tigers, closely resembled more familiar European creatures such as wolves or dogs. Heraldic beasts made their appearance on shields, on the crests of helmets, and on wood and stone carvings.

HORSE

The prancing horse appears prominently in heraldry, symbolizing speed, power and nobility. In the Christian tradition it represents courage. The black horse is a herald of death.

Heraldic Beasts

Heraldic Beasts

EAGLE
Noblest of birds, it rises above all, sees all and swoops swiftly on its prey.

GRIFFIN
Combining the eagle and lion, the griffin represents vigilance and vengeance.

COCKEREL
The heraldic cock represents pride, courage and alertness.

LION
King of beasts and beast of kings, the lion embodies valour, wisdom, energy and protective power.

UNICORN
This mythical beast represents purity, nobility and, with its prominent horn, male prowess. In heraldry it usually counterbalances the extrovert power of the lion.

DOGS, FOXES AND WOLVES

In most cultures the dog is a propitious symbol, standing for loyalty, watchfulness, courage, and skill in the hunt. In the Celtic tradition they are also associated with healing. Faithful in life, dogs were often sacrificed and buried along with their owners. The fox often symbolizes cunning and deceit, although Native Americans credit it with instinctive wisdom. In Christian tradition, wolves represent cruelty, devouring the sheep who refuse the protection of the Good Shepherd; but for the Romans the she-wolf who suckled Romulus and Remus symbolized maternal care.

Fox

In Oriental myth the fox is a powerfully positive symbol. In Japan it represents longevity and serves as the magical messenger of the rice god Inari. The Chinese credit the fox with the power to change shape and even assume human form.

Dogs, Foxes and Wolves

ANUBIS
The Egyptian guardian of the dead and god of mummification was shown as a jackal or jackal-headed man.

WEREWOLF
Human by day, savage beast by night, the were-wolf is a potent symbol of fear and the violence that lurks under the veneer of civilization.

CANIS MAJOR
The ancients saw a dog in the form of the constellation Canis Major. Sirius, the Dog Star, heralds summer's long, hot "dog days".

CATS

Nocturnal and independent, the cat was domesticated by the ancient Egyptians *c*.2000BCE and came to represent the goddess Bastet. The Chinese credited the cat with the ability to banish evil spirits, although its entry into a house was seen as an omen of poverty. In the West, the cat represented Satan, lust and darkness, and its best-known symbolic appearance is as the black familiar of the witch. In their more favourable aspect, cats were seen as rainmakers, perhaps owing to their sensitivity to water.

Cats

BASTET
To the Egyptians. the cat stood for Bastet, goddess of love, sex and fertility.

JAGUAR
South American traditions see a jaguar's reflective eyes as paths to the spirit realm.

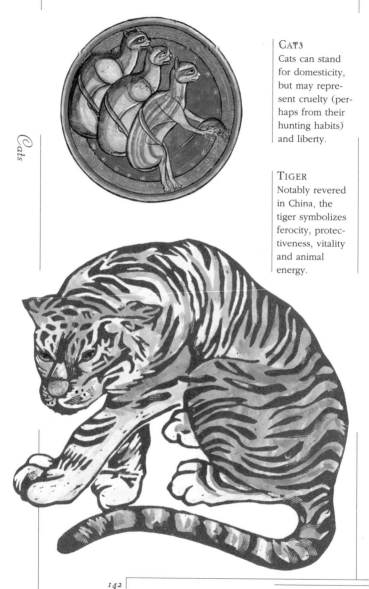

Cats

CATS
Cats can stand for domesticity, but may represent cruelty (perhaps from their hunting habits) and liberty.

TIGER
Notably revered in China, the tiger symbolizes ferocity, protectiveness, vitality and animal energy.

BIRDS AND FLIGHT

Flight represents freedom from the physical restrictions of earth-bound life, and the ascent of the soul to the gods, either through mystical experience or death. Birds share some of these symbolic meanings. They can also assume the role of messengers from higher powers, whether for good or ill. One dark and one light-coloured bird in the branches of the Tree of Life represent the dual nature of reality (darkness and light, life and death). In a Hindu variant, one bird eats the tree's fruit while the other watches, symbolizing the active life in contrast to the contemplative.

ICARUS
Icarus represents the fate of over-weening ambition. He and his father Daedalus flew on wings attached with wax. But Icarus flew too close to the sun: the wax melted and he fell to his death.

Birds and Flight

PELICAN

The old belief that the pelican shed its own blood to feed its young made it a symbol of self-sacrifice and, in Christian tradition, of Christ. In alchemy the bird represents resurrection.

RAVEN

The raven was credited with the gift of prophecy, often of an unwelcome kind. Its appearance is sometimes said to presage death.

FEATHERS

For Native Americans, feathers symbolize the Great Spirit and the sun. For the Celts, a feathered cloak gave lightness, speed and an ability to visit other worlds.

LEDA AND THE SWAN

In Greek myth, Zeus took the form of a swan to seduce Queen Leda of Sparta, and the swan therefore came to symbolize love and the gods. It also stands for solitude, music and poetry, and its whiteness represents sincerity.

Birds and Flight

PEACOCK

This bird represented the risen Christ – its flesh was once said to be incorruptible.

BA

The Egyptians believed that the soul, or *ba*, could flit between this world and the next, and depicted it as a hawk with the head of the deceased.

FISHES AND SHELLS

Fishes and Shells

Many cultures see the fish as a symbol of fecundity and the life-giving properties of water. Fish represent life in the depths and thus stand for inspiration and creativity. In Greek, the first letters of *Iesous CHristos, THeou 'Uios, Soter* (Jesus Christ, Son of God, Saviour) make the word *ichthus*, "fish", and there is a strong symbolic association of Christ with fish. In Buddhism the fish symbolizes freedom from desire and attachment. The Hindu gods Brahma and Vishnu sometimes appear in fish form. Universally feminine, the shell stands for birth, good fortune and resurrection.

THE BIRTH OF VENUS
The association between the scallop and the goddess Venus is the theme of this famous painting of *c.*1480 by Botticelli. In myth, Venus was born from the foam produced when the severed genitals of the god Uranus were cast into the sea. The goddess was carried ashore on a scallop shell.

SALMON
Its ability to find distant spawning grounds links the fish with prophecy and inspiration in Celtic myth.

Fishes and Shells

THREE FISHES
Sometimes depicted as intertwined and sometimes sharing a single head, the three fishes are a symbol of the Holy Trinity in Christian tradition.

MIRACULOUS DRAUGHT OF FISHES
The symbol of abundance and wisdom. Luke's account of Christ's miracle predicts Peter's later role as a "fisher of men".

Fishes and Shells

JONAH

Jonah was swallowed by "a great fish", but emerged after three days and nights. Christians see the episode as prefiguring Christ's death and resurrection.

CONCH

The sound of the conch symbolizes the voice of Buddha. To Hindus the shell is sacred to Vishnu.

OCTOPUS

Representing creation unfolding from the mystic centre, it can be linked with the sign of Cancer.

MONKEYS AND ELEPHANTS

Monkeys and elephants figure extensively in Eastern symbolism. The monkey, which seems to chatter incessantly and fruitlessly, represents the distracted mind that must be focused by practices such as meditation: when tamed, the monkey is capable of great loyalty.

The symbolism of the elephant derives from the animal's important role in civil and commercial life. Traditionally the vehicle for princes and maharajahs who rode high upon its back, the elephant represents status, strength and foresight. Because of its longevity, it stands for victory over death, and wisdom and dignity in old age.

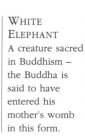

Monkeys and Elephants

WHITE ELEPHANT
A creature sacred in Buddhism – the Buddha is said to have entered his mother's womb in this form.

MYSTIC MONKEYS
This trio – See No Evil, Hear No Evil and Speak no Evil – symbolizes our ability to rise above gossip and spite. and to control and discipline our minds.

Monkeys and Elephants

HANUMAN

The Hindu monkey god, a hero of the *Ramayana*, symbolizes loyalty (to Lord Rama), strength and cunning. He tames fire, symbolizing the tantric power to turn fierce emotions into spiritual energy.

GANESHA

The Hindu elephant-god of sacred wisdom, invincibility and prudence, Ganesha is a patron of learning. He is often shown as elephant-headed, with four arms to confer blessings.

SHEEP AND GOATS

For many in the West, the goat is primarily a symbol of Satan and magic, but outside the Judeo–Christian tradition it enjoys a more positive image. In ancient Greece it was sacred to Zeus (who as an infant was suckled by the goat-nymph Amalthea), while its fecundity and cunning rendered it sacred also to Pan and Artemis. Perhaps because of its mountain home, the goat in the Hindu tradition symbolized superiority and the higher self. In Norse legend Thor's chariot was pulled across the heavens by goats.

The sheep usually stands for the opposite – blindness and stupidity. But its tendency to follow unquestioningly has also made it a symbol of the devoted disciple who surrenders individual will in exchange for salvation.

DEVIL
This depiction of the goat as Devil by Eliphas Lévi (see page 245) incorporates a range of magical symbolism. Thus the caduceus (see page 136) rises from the genitals and the pentagram occupies the place of the third eye.

Sheep and Goats

Sheep and Goats

GOOD SHEPHERD

Derived from pagan images of Orpheus, the Good Shepherd who cares for and protects the helpless was a common symbol of Christ in early Christian art.

GOAT-FISH

Ea, the Babylonian god of the waters, is often portrayed as a goat–fish, a symbol uniting the power of sea and land. The image below, based on Sumerian pottery, shows Ea as four goats around a central symbol for water.

PASCHAL LAMB

The lamb sacrificed at Passover represents obedience to God. For Christians the lamb is Jesus, sacrificed for us.

BULLS, STAGS AND BEARS

To the modern mind the bull may seem an unambiguous representation of maleness, strength and procreative power. In the Mithraic cult of Roman times it was sacrificed at the turn of the year, its blood symbolizing the masculine essence that fertilized the feminine earth. But the symbolism of the bull is actually not so clear-cut. The crescent shape of its horns has marked it as a lunar rather than a solar animal, particularly among the civilizations of the Mediterranean and the Near East. As such, it carries feminine connotations, and was attributed by the Romans to the goddess Venus.

OX
In Daoism the ox represents the ego. The sage Laozi is often shown riding an ox to indicate the possibility of taming the ego.

STAG
Shamans have often been depicted dressed as stags, indicating its role as a symbol of wisdom. In Mediterranean cultures the stag was identified with the Tree of Life.

Bulls, Stags and Bears

EUROPA
Zeus took the form of a white bull to abduct Europa. Christian interpretations saw this as Christ carrying the soul to heaven.

BEAR
Bears symbolize strength and bravery to Native Americans and Chinese. They were sacred to the Greek goddess Artemis.

SWINE

The pig features prominently in the symbology of many civilizations. Owing to the large size of her litters and her numerous teats, the sow was a symbol of fertility throughout the ancient world. The Egyptians believed the white sow to be sacred to Isis, the great mother goddess, while the black pig was attributed to Seth, the sinister god of disruption. In some Greek legends, Zeus was suckled by a sow while in hiding from his father Cronos, and pigs were routinely sacrificed to Demeter (the Roman Ceres), goddess of the fertility of the earth. Hindus also respect the sow, and hold it to symbolize Vajravarahi, the feminine

GLUTTONY
The pig represents gluttony, one of the Seven Deadly Sins, abhorred by the Church because it strengthened the coarser, material side of human nature and also symbolized selfishness and disregard of the needy.

Swine

Swine

SOW
With her large litter, the sow is an apt symbol of fecundity and motherhood.

BOAR
In Celtic legends, boars stand for magic, metamorphosis and prophecy.

aspect of the god Vishnu (who himself was once incarnated as a boar). Buddhists see the pig as a symbol of ignorance and greed, while it represents uncleanness in the Judaic tradition and may not be eaten (perhaps originally for good hygienic reasons). Christians adopted the pig as a sign of impurity and sinfulness: Christ drives a host of demons from a possessed man into a herd of swine, symbolizing the need for humans to triumph over their lower natures.

LESSER CREATURES

The smaller animals were also felt to play an important part in the magical world which our ancestors saw around them. Living close to nature, the ancients felt all things to be interconnected in an intricate web of being, and they attributed meaning to all aspects of nature. Consciousness was thought to pervade the whole of creation – the stars in the night sky, the wind in the trees, even the scurryings of the smallest creatures. The insects developed particularly rich symbolic associations. For example, flies were considered to be driven by demonic forces: Beelzebub, a name now synonymous with Satan, was originally a Syrian personification of the destructive power of swarming insects.

SPIDER
Spiders stand for the Great Mother in her devouring aspect. For the Celts, their webs symbolized the web that held all life together. For Egyptians and Greeks the web stood for fate; for Christians it represented Satan's snare.

Lesser Creatures

BAT
In many cultures the bat embodies the powers of darkness and chaos. Buddhists see it as a symbol of the ever-distracted mind. In China it represented long life and happiness.

TOAD
Associated with witches, the toad is often depicted with a jewel in its head, denoting wisdom.

HARE
Widely held to symbolize love, fertility and the menstrual cycle, hares are closely associated with the moon.

HYBRID CREATURES

Imaginary hybrid creatures have two main functions: they bring together the symbolic strengths of different animals; and may represent the fundamental unity of existence. For example, the chimera – part lion, part goat, part serpent – symbolized the three divisions of the year – spring, summer and winter. To the minds that invented them, hybrids presented no inherent contradictions, because if all creation was interconnected, there was no reason why certain ingredients should not be permutated in new and different ways. There is much evidence that the ancients did not separate imagination and reality in the way that is habitual to

GARUDA
Half-man and half-eagle, Garuda appears in Hinduism as the vehicle of the great god Vishnu. Devotees of Vishnu use images of Garuda, enemy of the *naga*s (snake demons), as their emblem.

Hybrid Creatures

Hybrid Creatures

SPHINX
In Greek myth,
the Sphinx had
a woman's head
and breasts, a
lion's body and
eagle's wings.
The Greeks gave
the same name
to the Egyptian
sphinx, a man-
headed lion.

us. If something could be imagined, there was a sense in which it must exist.

Most hybrids carried a positive symbolic meaning. They inhabited a dimension that spanned this and other worlds, and thus could serve not only to help humankind in the struggle against dark forces but also to act as messengers from the gods and as sources of wisdom in themselves.

BASILISK
Part cock and part serpent, the desert-dwelling basilisk or cockatrice could kill with its terrifying gaze.

Hybrid Creatures

SATYR
Nature spirits and followers of Dionysus (the Greek god of ecstasy, wine and music), the satyrs were half men and half goats. Christians later identified them with Satan.

CHIMERA
An ancient Greek symbol of elemental chaos and the dangers of land and sea. It was a portent of storms, shipwrecks and natural disasters, and appears in medieval art as a symbol of Satanic forces.

Hybrid Creatures

HARPY

In Greek mythology, Harpies were female wind spirits. They could summon winds, causing storms on land and whirlpools at sea, and were believed to be responsible for sudden deaths.

MERMAID

Sometimes said to be hallucinations by sailors starved of female company, mermaids symbolize idealized, elusive feminine beauty, but also vanity and fickleness.

SIREN

The Sirens stood for feminine beauty in its most beguiling and destructive form. Depicted as birds with women's heads, they possessed beautiful voices which, heard above the sighing of the sea, lured mariners to their doom.

Hybrid Creatures

CENTAUR

Part man, part horse, the centaur represents the wild, lawless and instinctual side of human nature. However, the wise Chiron, tutor of the hero Herakles and gentlest of the centaurs, symbolized the healing powers of nature.

THE NATURAL WORLD

The direct experience of nature was the most powerful influence on the perceptions of the ancients. Their concepts of space and time, and of their own position in the universe, could be understood only in relation to the natural world, every aspect of which was believed to express a particular feature of divine energy. The earliest gods were, not surprisingly, embodiments of natural forces. Nearly all ancient cultures originally represented the earth and nature as a great mother goddess – for example: Neith (Egyptian), Gaia (Greek), Nokomis (Algonquin) and Danu (Celtic). Also widespread was the belief that all forms of life were interchangeable and that humankind was a part of nature, rather than its master. In depictions of the

CHRYSANTHE-MUM
In the East a symbol of good fortune and contemplation.

MYSTICAL GARDEN
The visionary 19th-century artist Samuel Palmer represents the garden as the enclosed, feminine principle (right).

The Natural World

Mesopotamian shepherd god Dumuzi (Tammuz), plant, animal and human forms blend into one another. Images of the tree-man (see page 172) occur in numerous Western cultures.

Although the primitive nature gods were often superseded by more sophisticated pantheons, myths and symbols based on the natural world remained prominent in all cultures, and some were of worldwide significance. The relationship between the bird (a symbol of heaven, fire, purity and the spirit) and the serpent (the earth and underworld) is the subject of numerous myths. And the turtle is a symbol of the universe (the heavens, earth and underworld represented by its upper shell, body and lower shell) in both North America and southern Asia. Depictions of the Tree of Life (see page 170) appear in nearly all cultures at all times, and this ancient symbol appears in modern Christianity as an emblem of the Virgin Mary, who gave the world her fruit, Jesus Christ.

TREES

The tree is one of humankind's most potent symbols. It is the embodiment of life, the point of union of the three realms (heaven, earth and water), and an axis around which the entire cosmos is organized. Ancient peoples widely believed trees to possess an abundance of divine creative energy (often personified in the form of supernatural creatures) which could be harnessed by the adept to allow access to other states of being. Forests came to symbolize mystery and transformation, and were home to sorcerers and enchanters.

Tree worship was widespread in nearly all parts of the globe where trees grew. Some tree symbols are virtually worldwide. For example, evergreens universally stand for longevity and immortality, while deciduous trees represent regeneration and rebirth. Individual species generally acquired their own, culture-specific significance. The

PALM TREE
Growing tall and with radiating foliage, the palm tree came to represent the sun and fame. Jewish and Christian tradition links palm leaves with the victorious coming of the Messiah. They were also funerary emblems of the afterlife.

Trees

Trees

oak was revered by the Celtic and Norse peoples, and in Greece, the elder was sacred to Pan, the bay to Apollo, the laurel to Dionysus. In Egypt, the tamarisk was sacred to Osiris.

Many trees were believed to have healing properties; thus aspen was used in the treatment of fevers. Hazel was thought to possess magical powers, and was used for water divining and magicians' wands.

FOREST
The forest is a place of darkness, chaos and uncertainty, in contrast to the order and openness of cultivated land. To those who show no fear, however, it may be a place of peace and refuge. Psychologically, it is a symbol of the unconscious mind.

PINE CONE
Its shape and erect appearance made it a sign of masculinity for the Greeks.

CHRISTMAS TREE
In northern Europe the decorated evergreen symbolized life persisting even in midwinter.

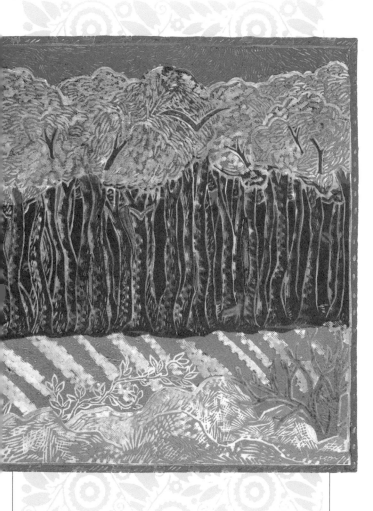

Trees

TREE OF LIFE
The tree in the centre of Eden represents perfect harmony, its fruit the riches of spiritual growth, such as truth, love and wisdom.

WORLD TREE
With its roots around the earth and its branches in the heavens, the World Tree symbolizes the potential ascent of humankind from the realm of matter to the rarefied reaches of the spirit.

INVERTED TREE
With its roots in the heavens and growing down toward the earth, it symbolizes the creative power of the spirit and the belief that human life is the descent of spirit into bodily form. This Kabbalistic inverted Tree of Life shows the Sefiroth – the ten aspects of God.

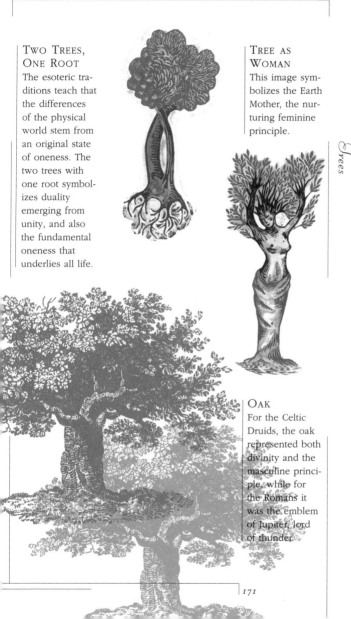

TWO TREES, ONE ROOT

The esoteric traditions teach that the differences of the physical world stem from an original state of oneness. The two trees with one root symbolizes duality emerging from unity, and also the fundamental oneness that underlies all life.

TREE AS WOMAN

This image symbolizes the Earth Mother, the nurturing feminine principle.

Trees

OAK

For the Celtic Druids, the oak represented both divinity and the masculine principle, while for the Romans it was the emblem of Jupiter, lord of thunder.

171

Trees

TREE AS MAN

This potent fertility symbol, also called the Green Man, stands for the male energy which impregnates the female earth but is itself subject to the cycle of decay and renewal.

TREE OF KNOWLEDGE

The "knowledge" is that of good and evil. After illicitly tasting its fruit, Adam and Eve were driven from paradise forever to confront the world of dualities. In addition to its familiar role as tempter, the entwined serpent is an ancient mystical symbol of rising earth energy.

FLOWERS AND PLANTS

The Greeks believed that paradise was carpeted with asphodels. The Chinese imagined that for each woman living in this world, a flower bloomed in the next. These two ancient beliefs exemplify the most common symbolic meanings of flowers: the paradisal state and feminine beauty. The opening of the flower from the bud represents creation and the energy of the sun. Flowers are universal symbols of youth and vitality, but because of their impermanence they also connote fragility and transience.

Plants represent the cycle of life (fertility, death and rebirth). Many herbs were considered sacred, some because of their medicinal properties and others because their growth habit or appearance suggested a link with the gods or humans (for example, a mandrake root resembles the human form).

MANDRAKE
The mandrake root was believed to have great healing powers. In Hebrew tradition it symbolized fertility and was eaten to aid conception.

Flowers and Plants

Flowers and Plants

MISTLETOE
Mistletoe was taken to symbolize the female in relation to the maleness of the oak in whose branches it grew.

ROSE
In Christianity the red rose can symbolize the Virgin Mary, or the blood shed by Christ on the cross.

GARLAND
Combining the symbolism of flower and ring, garlands represent good luck, holiness, fertility, initiation and, in the form of the funerary wreath, the union of life and death.

LOTUS
Emerging into sunlight out of muddy depths, the lotus symbolizes the path to enlightenment.

GARLIC
A symbol of the higher world, partly because of its link with lightning (traditionally said to smell like garlic).

GARDEN

A symbol of
nature under
control and of
the human soul,
which must be
cared for and
cultivated.

HERBS

Many herbs
have symbolic
meanings, for
example rue
(repentance)
and thyme
(purity).

Flowers and Plants

FOOD AND DRINK

Food and Drink

Food connotes fertility, abundance and celebration and is often linked with peace and the resolution of differences. This association stems from a belief that food puts us in touch with the source of the life-force, creating a universal fellowship. In many cultures it was seen as a breach of natural law to harm a person with whom one had broken bread.

Drink is also potently symbolic. Water, the primordial fluid, suggests life and purity, while milk represents the sustaining compassion of the earth and motherhood. Wine is connected with blood, sacrifice and altered states.

HONEY
Together with milk, honey symbolizes the abundance of the Promised Land of the Israelites. It stands also for immortality and fertility.

SHEAVES OF CORN
A symbol of the earth's fertility and the spiritual ripeness of enlightenment. Ears of corn are said to be the offspring of the sun and earth.

FUNGI
Because of their phallic shape, toadstools were associated with male fertility. In China, the mushroom is a symbol of happiness and rebirth, and was said to be the food of the Daoist immortals.

POMEGRANATE
In Greece, the pomegranate was the symbol of Persephone and of the return of life in spring. In the Christian tradition, it symbolized God's boundless love.

Food and Drink

DIONYSUS
The Greek god of wine, revelry and agriculture, known to the Romans as Bacchus. He represents the union of heaven and earth, of spirit and sensuality. He presided over all altered states, such as drunkenness, religious ecstasy and acting. He could appear as a man or woman.

PEACH
In China the peach symbolizes marriage, immortality and longevity. The god of long life is often shown emerging from, or holding, a peach of immortality from a tree in paradise that bears fruit every 3,000 years.

Food and Drink

LAST SUPPER

The last meal shared by Jesus and his disciples came to symbolize his sacrifice on the cross, repeated in the bread and wine of the Eucharist.

GOLDEN APPLE

A symbol of discord. Paris gave it to Aphrodite, angering other goddesses and leading to the Trojan War.

THE ELEMENTS

The Elements

The ancients believed the elements to be energy forces that sustained the world. In the West there were four: fire, water, air and earth. In the East there were five (metal in China; "ether", a spiritual element, in India and Tibet). The central importance of the elements as organizing principles in the universe is a constant in the symbology of all cultures. Alchemists represented each element as a triangle (see opposite). The elements made up all things, including the human body – flesh (earth), breath (air), heat (fire) and blood (water) – and one's physical and psychological health was a matter of keeping them in balance, just as a balance was needed in the outside world.

HUMAN BODY Composed of the four elements plus the invisible spiritual dimension, the (male) body was the universal symbol for life in all its forms, the link between heaven and earth, and the personification of the energy of the gods.

The Elements

SYLPH
A spirit of the air, believed to be in communion with the divine.

SALAMANDER
In Western traditions the spirit and guardian of fire, which lived in a volcano.

GNOME
A mischievous underground spirit of the earth, who needs to be appeased with offerings.

ONDINE
The female spirit of water, both captivating and treacherous.

AIR

ISIS
Egypt's greatest goddess, Isis is the divine mother and protector. In the form of a bird she fanned the breath of life into her dead brother Osiris.

SAILING SHIP
Many seafaring cultures had divine figures (such as the Greek Aeolus) who controlled the wind; sailors prayed to them before a voyage.

The Elements: Air

PRANA

For many Eastern philosophies, the vital energy of the cosmos is carried in the air. Symbolized by the central character, above, it is called *prana* by Hindus and *qi* by the Chinese.

PEGASUS

The winged horse symbolizes our desire to take to the air – and, as Bellerophon discovered when he fell from it – the folly of trying to tame the elements.

183

FIRE

PHOENIX
Mythical symbol
of resurrection
and immortality,
it perishes in
flames every
hundred years,
to rise anew
from the ashes.

AGNI
The early Hindu
god Agni (Fire)
personifies the
holy fire that is
seen as the cos-
mic witness of
all key rites and
sacrifices.

INCENSE
In the East, incense is believed to purify and to protect against evil spirits.

SMOKE
To Native Americans it stands for peace and our path at death.

The Elements: Fire

SHIP BURIAL
Vikings cremated their chiefs in longships, the spirit rising in the smoke to the sun, giver of life.

LANTERN
A lucky symbol on a Chinese lantern was said to bestow fortune on anything its shadow touched.

FIRECRACKER
In China, fire-crackers bring luck and frighten demons. They are lit in groups of three to honour the gods of health, wealth and longevity.

WATER

RIVERS
Rivers represent the life-force, passing time and the frontier between life and death. For Hindus, the Ganges can purify all shortcomings.

The Elements: Water

STEAM
Water ascending as steam is the transformation of the material into the spiritual. Native Americans attribute to steam the combined purifying powers of fire and water, and use it in the purifying sweat lodge ceremony.

PROMETHEUS
In Greek myth, Prometheus (left) stole fire (a symbol of the wisdom that divides divinity from humanity) from the gods, and brought it to earth. He symbolizes the courage needed to challenge the gods' decree.

STREAMS
Similar to rivers, but closer to the creative source. Four streams flowed from the root of the Tree of Life in Paradise.

WELLS
Water drawn from underground usually represents a sacred gift from the womb of earth. Many are credited with healing power.

The Elements: Water

BOATS

Boats or rafts symbolize a safe passage to death, enlightenment or salvation. Christ walked on the water, and many cultures have legends of holy men and women sailing in the most unlikely craft. Patrick, the patron saint of Ireland, is said to have used a stone raft, while Bodhidharma (left), who brought Zen Buddhism to China, crossed the Yangzi on a hollow reed.

ICE AND SNOW

Ice symbolizes sterility, coldness and rigidity. Snow shares something of this symbolism, but being white it also stands for truth and purity.

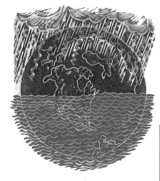

The Elements: Water

CLOUDS AND MIST

Clouds symbolize mystery and the sacred. The Chinese believed that clouds were formed from the union of yin and yang and symbolized peace.

POSEIDON

Poseidon (Neptune to the Romans) symbolized the elemental power of the sea; it was he who granted or withheld safe passage to mariners.

RAIN

As a life-giving blessing from heaven, rain has always symbolized divine favour and revelation, the descent of grace upon the earth.

EARTH

VOLCANO

Volcanoes are terrifying examples of the earth's destructive energy. In Greek myth, volcanic activity was a sign that Hephaistos, the smith god, was busy in his workshop.

PAGODA

The Chinese and Japanese form of the Buddhist stupa, or relic monument, the pagoda represents ascent to enlightenment, and traditionally has seven levels to mark the stages of this ascent. It also stands for Mount Meru, the world axis at the centre of the universe.

The Elements: Earth

VALLEY
A protective feminine symbol associated with fertility, cultivation and water. In Christian tradition it is linked with darkness, the unknown and death.

MOUNTAIN
The meeting-places of heaven and earth, mountains symbolize masculinity, eternity, and ascent from animal to spiritual nature. Mountain tops are often said to be the home of the gods.

CAVE
Another feminine symbol, the cave can represent the entrance to the underworld, the heart of the world, initiation, the unconscious, or the path to esoteric wisdom.

RAINBOWS

To the ancients, who believed that all celestial phenomena were signs of divine activity, the appearance of a rainbow in the wake of a fierce storm signified the presence of a benign deity. Because it appeared to span the divide between the heavens and the earth, the rainbow was a potent symbol of divine communication. The Incas associated it with their sun god, while in ancient Greece it was personified by the goddess Iris, who carried messages to mortals from the gods on Mount Olympus. In Nilo-Saharan Africa, kings and priests claimed descent

RAINBOW BODY

In the Hindu and Buddhist Tantric traditions, the rainbow body is the highest meditative state. The body dissolves symbolically into rainbow light and earthly life is shown to be truly insubstantial.

Rainbows

NOAH'S RAINBOW

In Judeo-Christian tradition, the rainbow symbolizes God's forgiveness and his covenant with humankind following the great Flood. According to the Book of Genesis, a rainbow appeared in the sky after Noah's ark came to rest on land after the deluge (see page 35).

from rainbows to justify their elevated social status. In some African societies, the rainbow is the sky serpent, a beneficent symbol of energy flowing between heaven and earth. Such positive associations are also evident in European folklore, which maintains that a crock of gold can be found where a rainbow meets the earth.

The rainbow is sometimes a bridge between this world and that of the gods. The Norse gods are said to have built a rainbow bridge called Bifrost between their dwelling, Asgard, and the earth.

THUNDER AND LIGHTNING

Thunder and Lightning

Thunder and lightning were once almost universally interpreted as manifestations of the gods, and most commonly as expressions of divine wrath. The Chinese goddess Tian Mou was the embodiment of lightning, whose task was to illuminate evildoers so that they could be struck down by the thunder god. Native Americans attributed thunder and lightning to the universal spirit, the Thunderbird. In Greek myth, Semele asked Zeus to come to her undisguised; he appeared as a bolt of lightning that consumed her by fire. In the Jewish and Christian traditions the phenomena of thunder and lightning herald God's presence.

LIGHTNING Associated with intuition and inspiration. In shamanic tradition, to be struck by lightning is a mark of initiation, and to be killed by it is to be taken directly to the heavens. In the West, some believe a lightning strike awakens psychic powers.

Thunder and Lightning

DORJE
The Tibetan Buddhist thunderbolt sceptre used in rituals and magic, the *dorje* represents male energy, its two globes symbolizing the meeting of heaven and earth.

THOR
The Norse thunder god rumbled across the heavens in his wagon and hurled his hammer to produce thunderbolts. A hammer symbol was used to protect houses from fire.

SHAMAN
Shamans are depicted in the zigzag shape of a lightning flash, symbolizing their ability to cross the bridge dividing the worlds.

DAY AND NIGHT

In Christian, Buddhist and Islamic cultures, light is an aspect of divinity and kingship, and daytime is associated with divine activity and creation, as in the "seven days" in which God created the world and the "day of Brahma", the eons-long cycle of manifestations of the Hindu creator god. In the Hindu religion, day (symbolizing spirit) and night (representing matter) are believed to be brought about by the opening and closing of Shiva's eyes. In European cultures, day generally stands for life and night for death, with the dawn corresponding to resurrection and joy.

Night was the time when the spirits of the dead walked the earth and the "powers of darkness" were abroad. As Christianity spread, pagans were forced to perform their rituals covertly at night in order to avoid persecution, reinforcing the negative symbolism of night. As late as the 17th century it was held that

Day and Night

diseases were more readily contracted at night, and tales of the nocturnal transformations of men and women into werewolves and vampire bats were widely believed. But night was not universally negative: it could stand for rest from the toils of the day, and for the womb of mother nature, which opened to readmit her children after sunset.

SLEEP
In many cultures sleep is when the soul leaves the body and travels in other levels of reality.

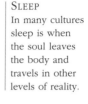

Day and Night

NURSE OF THE GODS
In Greece and Mesopotamia, she represented the dawn and the end of time.

FLAMING CAULDRON
For Zoroastrians, this is the symbol of Ahura Mazda, the bringer of light.

197

JEWELS AND PRECIOUS METALS

Jewels and Precious Metals

Decorative and durable, jewels and precious metals have been used for centuries as talismans and amulets, and have acquired rich symbolic associations. A horde of gold and jewels hidden in a cave guarded by a dragon or serpent commonly represents the spiritual wisdom buried in the unconscious. In many religions a gem signifies a particular deity or holy person: in Christianity, for example, quartz stands for the Virgin Mary. Cut gemstones symbolize the revelation of the soul after the dross of the body has been chipped away: the sparkling facets denote the soul's reflection of the divine light.

Gemstones can also have negative connotations. In Christian legend, they were formed when Lucifer fell from heaven, his angelic light shattering into

LAPIS LAZULI
Prized as a mark of divine favour, success and talent, lapis lazuli is also associated with unselfish love and compassion. For the Chinese, the stone symbolized vision and the power to cure diseases of the eye. In ancient Mesopotamia, lapis lazuli symbolized the firmament and was used to decorate the ceilings of temples.

millions of lustrous fragments that stand for the inherent evil of material possessions. Fairies used gold and rubies to entice mortals away from home and family at night; the victims found the "treasure" turned into dead leaves in the cold light of day. The ambivalence of gem symbolism is exemplified in the Eastern belief that jewels were formed from the saliva of snakes, representing both venom and spiritual wisdom.

In many traditions, gold and silver were solidifications of solar and lunar energies respectively. Gold remains always untarnished, like the sun, while silver is subject to imperfections, like the face of the moon.

PEARL
The pearl has lunar, feminine, associations. Its origin within the shell of an oyster has caused it to be linked with hidden knowledge and esoteric wisdom. Pearls also symbolize patience, purity and peace, and tears of either sorrow or joy.

AGATE
A symbol of worldly success and happiness, agate also attracts sympathy for the wearer.

Jewels and Precious Metals

Jewels and Precious Metals

GOLD AND SILVER

Revered for its incorruptibility, gold is a near-universal symbol of the sun, divinity, purity, immortality, wisdom and masculinity. Silver, a lunar, feminine symbol, stands for virginity and eloquence. Polished silver represents the soul cleansed of sin. It is ambivalent in Christianity, in which pieces of silver symbolized Christ's betrayal.

JADE

The most precious stone to the Chinese, for whom it symbolized perfection, immortality and magical powers, all embodied in the Emperor. Heaven was often represented as a perforated jade disc.

RUBY

This gemstone symbolizes royalty, power, passion and Mars.

DIAMOND

Associated with permanence, incorruptibility, the sun and light.

EMERALD

A symbol of fertility, rain, wisdom, faith and Jupiter.

SAPPHIRE

Symbolizes the blue of the heavens and the heavenly virtues – truth, contemplation, chastity.

SUN, MOON AND STARS

The skies for ancient peoples were a screen on which they projected their most profound speculations and spiritual needs. As the prime source of light and heat, the sun combined with rain to bring forth and sustain life. Because of its high position in the heavens and the clarity of its light, the sun was regarded as all-seeing, and was worshipped as a (mostly masculine) god in a number of civilizations. To the Incas, the sun was a divine ancestor, whose temples were lavishly decorated with gold, the colour with which the sun was closely associated. Even in Christianity the sun was felt to be a worthy symbol of God. For Hindus, the sun symbolizes humankind's higher self, and Hindu scriptures speak of the soul after death ascending by the sun's rays towards the sun itself. The moon is

PARASOL
In ancient India those of high rank were shielded from the sun by parasols. In Buddhism it is a symbol of the Buddha when he was the highborn Prince Siddhartha, before he abandoned earthly wealth to pursue his destiny to attain enlightenment.

Sun, Moon and Stars

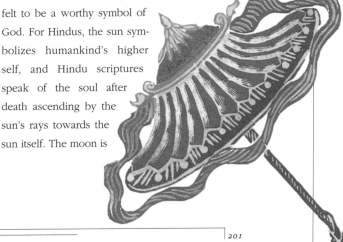

Sun, Moon and Stars

generally seen as feminine, partly owing to the association with the menstrual cycle. Constantly changing from phase to phase and varying its position in the sky, the moon is capricious in character, but at the same time symbolizes resurrection, immortality and the cyclical nature of all things. It stands for the power of the dark, mysterious side of nature, and the moon goddess was almost universally perceived as the weaver of fate and the controller of destinies, in the same way that she controlled the tides, the weather, rainfall and the seasons.

While the sun and moon symbolized the principal gods, the stars embodied those of lesser importance, whose influence on human fate was more remote.

WINGED SUN DISK
This symbolizes the majesty of the Egyptian sun god, ruler of the skies and creator of the world. The pharaohs considered themselves his sons.

PLOUGH (BIG DIPPER)
This constellation was taken to represent the energy that broke up the primal unity of existence into the diversity of creation.

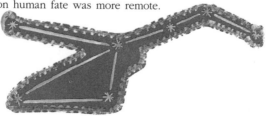

DAWN

Although the sun has masculine associations, dawn is usually seen as female. In Greek myth it was personified as Eos (Aurora to the Romans), sister of the sun god Helios and moon goddess Selene. Eos is depicted rising from the sea or traversing the sky in a chariot.

COMET

Comets traditionally were seen as manifestations of divine anger or as bringers of disaster, war and pestilence.

Sun, Moon and Stars

FULL MOON
Representing the plenitude of female energy, it echoes the symbolism of the circle to signify wholeness, completion and achievement.

NEW MOON
A symbol of ascent from the underworld (below). The crescent moon is an attribute of the Egyptian mother goddess Isis and of the Virgin Mary.

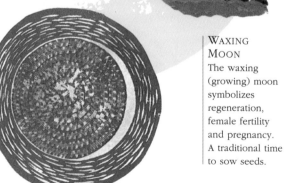

WAXING MOON
The waxing (growing) moon symbolizes regeneration, female fertility and pregnancy. A traditional time to sow seeds.

HUMAN
AND SPIRITUAL
SYMBOLS

Most esoteric traditions regard matter and spirit as opposites that come together only in humankind. The human spirit is considered to be a fragment of the universal energy, the divine principle: it defines our special relationship with God and differentiates us from the animal. Different cultures see the precise relationship between the human body and spirit very differently, and the way in which these opposites are reconciled is reflected in every aspect of life.

Christian theology emphasizes the split between spirituality and physicality: the body is seen as a vehicle for the soul or spirit, which represents the "true" person. The soul is an immortal gift of

SCALLOP
Echoing the form of the female pudenda, the scallop symbolizes the feminine principle, sexual passion, fertility and marriage. It is linked with the goddess Venus (see page 146).

Human and Spiritual Symbols

Human and Spiritual Symbols

God, which is joined with the body only temporarily for the duration of a life

Eastern and occult belief systems, in contrast, emphasize the interaction between body and spirit, and the essence of humanity – the soul – is a product of both spirit and matter. Certain forms of Hinduism and Buddhism recognize focal points, or *chakra*s within the body, where spiritual and bodily energies interact. Similarly, Chinese acupuncturists can manipulate the life-force, or *qi* (*ch'i*), which is believed to flow through the body along specific pathways called meridians, by inserting needles or applying pressure at certain points. A combination of physical and spiritual goals is also evident in yoga, a system of Indian philosophy.

Much of the symbolism of the body is common to East and West. For example, the belief that we were created in the image of God is echoed in depictions of the human being as microcosm, the universe in miniature.

CREATION
Creation myths are perhaps the most important myths in all cultures because they set out humankind's relationship with the gods and the cosmos. God's creation of humanity was a popular theme in medieval Christian art (right).

Sex and Fertility

To the ancients, sexuality was not merely a source of pleasure and a way of reproducing the species. The union of male and female energies in order to produce life was symbolic of all acts of creation, including the fertilization of the land, and even symbolized creation itself. In the Indian cult of Tantra, the cosmos was based on the union of the male principle (the god Shiva, often represented by the phallic *lingam*) with the female (the goddess Shakti, symbolized by the *yoni*, or vulva).

Explicit sexual symbols also appear in the art and myth of pre-Christian Europe, though they are linked more to fertility or ribald pleasure than to spiritual enlightenment. For example, in ancient Greece, Priapus, the god of fertility and sexual potency, was depicted as a man with an enormous phallus. His

ARTEMIS
A deity of birth and fertility and symbol of nature in all its aspects.

CORN DOLL
Fashioned from corn stalks and ears, the corn doll was used as a fertility talisman by women wishing for pregnancy.

LINGAM
A symbol of the masculine creative energy embodied by the Hindu god Shiva, the *lingam* stands for regeneration.

female counterpart, Baubo, a maidservant of the goddess Demeter, was similarly grotesque, appearing as a face on top of an enlarged vulva.

The natural world is a rich source of fertility symbols: fecund animals, such as the hare and frog, represent regeneration. The egg, which carries new life and resembles the testicles, stands for the continuity of life. In some Christian traditions, eggs are associated with Easter and the resurrection of Christ; and in the mythologies of Egypt, Japan, India, Polynesia and Scandinavia it is said that the world itself originated from a primal egg.

Sex and Fertility

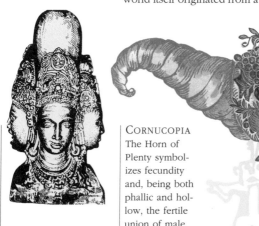

CORNUCOPIA
The Horn of Plenty symbolizes fecundity and, being both phallic and hollow, the fertile union of male and female.

Sex and Fertility

MAYPOLE
Spring fertility rituals of many cultures feature dancing around a decorated pole – a phallic symbol representing the annual awakening of nature. At a deeper level it symbolizes the world axis (see page 167).

PHALLIC GIANT
In much of Europe, as well as the Pacific islands, effigies of giants and nature spirits with erect phalluses were carved in wood and stone, or on hillsides (below). They represented fertility and masculine creative power.

WEDDING CAKE
This began as a way of wishing fertility on the bride and groom, as well as symbolising their union.

BODY, YOUTH AND AGE

Most cultures recognize three phases of human development – childhood, maturity and old age. The playfulness of childhood is symbolized in Hinduism by Krishna frolicking with the milkmaids, in Christianity by the boy Jesus asking questions of the learned men in the temple, and in ancient Egypt by the infant Horus (in the form of Harpocrates, "Horus the Child") listening to the voice of the universe. The achievements and duties of adulthood are embodied in the ministry of Christ, and in Greek myth by Theseus, who killed the Minotaur to

CLOTHES
Nakedness symbolizes purity and innocence but clothes are more ambivalent. Thus fine robes convey authority and privilege but also foolishness, pride, vanity and worldliness.

Body, Youth and Age

prevent the sacrifice of young lives. The wisdom of old age is symbolically expressed in the Greek god Cronos (the Roman Saturn), who ruled over the universe in the Golden Age, and in Christian depictions of God the Father as an old man. In most Eastern traditions, youth and age are seen as two complementary aspects – innocence and wisdom – of the one reality.

In many cultures the human body is a symbol of the indwelling soul. The ancient Egyptians mummified the body

JEWELRY
Jewelry can connote vanity, but gems often have their own positive meaning.

LOCKET
A lock of hair symbolizes its owner's life-force, especially if they are deceased.

so that the soul could could continue to reside in it after death. Buddhists, Hindus and medieval Christians revered the physical remains of departed saints. Native American and Siberian shamans are symbolically torn limb from limb on their inner initiatory journey, only to be revivified into a new wholeness.

But the body is also symbolically ambivalent. Although sacred, it is also

JUDGMENT OF PARIS
Beauty can be alluring but destructive. A gold apple inscribed "to the fairest" was claimed by three goddesses; Paris's choice of Venus led to the Trojan War, in which he died.

HAND
The right is associated with rectitude and the left with deviousness. Open and raised, the right hand may denote reassurance and freedom from fear.

FOOT
Feet represent stability and freedom. It was believed that they could draw energy from the ground. The Buddha's footprints (left) were said to bear marks denoting his great destiny.

HEART
The basic symbol for sincerity, love and compassion, it also represents the centre of things. Pierced by an arrow and surmounted by a cross or crown of thorns, it is a symbol of Christ.

profane, because it shares the lusts of the animal world. In many Western and Near Eastern traditions, the female body in particular has been a symbol of depravity, because of its power to divert men from their purpose, and the figure of the temptress appears in numerous myths, from the Sirens of ancient Greece to the German Lorelei (a water spirit whose singing lured sailors onto rocks).

SKELETON
Representing death and vanity, it can also stand for the renunciation of material comforts.

FATHER TIME
A symbol of impermanence and mortality, he may be depicted carrying a sickle or hourglass.

Body, Youth and Age

Good and Evil

GOOD AND EVIL

The antagonistic forces of good and evil are characteristically represented by irreconcilable opposites – courage versus cowardice, and so on. In Christian symbolism, few tread the straight and narrow path that leads to eternal life, the majority following the broad road to damnation. Good and evil are embodied respectively in God and Satan.

TAIJI (YIN AND YANG)
An ancient Chinese symbol of the opposing but complementary forces that constitute the cosmos.

In most cultures, the long-term rewards of goodness are symbolized as treasures worth pursuing, while the punishments attendant upon evil are truly horrifying. The Indic idea of *karma* is less final in its judgment,

DEMON
The Greek *daimon* originally meant a god, but in Christian times came to mean a nature spirit, and then an imp of Satan.

allowing unlimited opportunities for redemption. Every action is a cause that carries an equivalent effect, in this life or in another incarnation in this world.

However, many of the world's great esoteric traditions reject the idea of good and evil as opposites and teach that every action contains elements of both. For example, a doctor might inflict pain to treat a wound or a soldier take one life in order to save hundreds. Everyday existence depends upon the death of plants and animals, without which there can be no life. Thus, good and evil are not in conflict and indeed depend on one another.

Good and Evil

ANGEL
In Jewish and Christian tradition, angels symbolize the communication between God and humankind.

MONK AND NUN
Those who follow the solitary life symbolize piety, austerity and dedication to spiritual progress.

HALOES, MASKS AND SHADOWS

The halo is best known from its appearances in Christian iconography from the 2nd century onward, but it was a sign of divinity or holiness much earlier, featuring in ancient Greek and Eastern art. It stand for the sun and the divine radiance emanating from the individual. On the other hand, the shadow is a symbol of our material nature and represents an obscuring of the light of heaven.

The mask can stand for deceit and the artificial face that conceals a person's true nature. However, in shamanism and Tibetan Buddhism, it is believed that ritual masks can help an individual to relinquish the ego, allowing the spirits of helpful animals or gods to enter and work through him or her.

HALO
A symbol of divine radiance, wisdom and life-force. In Christian art, the halo is usually round, and white or golden in colour.

Haloes, Masks and Shadows

VARIATIONS ON THE HALO
A round halo may denotes a dead or martyred holy person. God the Father's halo is often triangular or diamond-shaped.

SHADOW
The symbol of materiality and, in Jungian psychology, of often unrecognized primal urges.

MANDORLA
This variant of the halo surrounds the entire body of a holy person. Symbolizing both power and spirituality, it often appears around Christ in paintings of the Ascension.

Haloes, Masks and Shadows

Haloes, Masks and Shadows

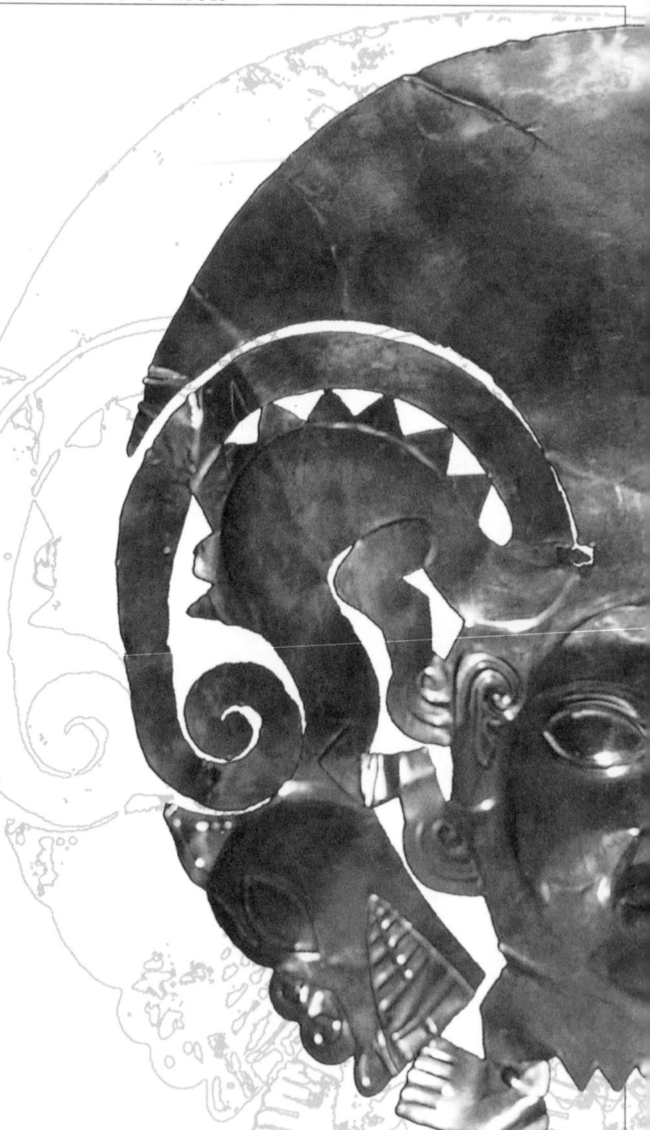

MASK
Suggesting transformation as well as concealment, masks may be used to put us in touch with gods, spirits and the instinctual wisdom of animals.

Haloes, Masks and Shadows

GODS AND GODDESSES

Early written records indicate that the ancients had a sophisticated appreciation of the forces that created and sustained life. However, the origin of these forces was beyond description or comprehension, so it was natural for people to present a rationalized, symbolic picture of ultimate realities. Jung believed that the human psyche has a "natural religious function", a pressing need to give conscious expression to unconscious archetypes (see page 15). In psychological terms, early peoples projected outward the archetype of higher powers, and thus emerged the concept of the gods – beings with all the qualities to which people aspired in their own lives. In many cultures the

GOD THE FATHER
In Christian art, God is usually depicted as a wise father figure with a long white beard (a symbol of dignity). However, before the 15th century such images were rare and paintings of biblical events usually showed God in the form of Christ.

Gods and Goddesses

gods proliferated, each symbolizing a particular aspect of nature (thunder, the sea, fire) or a human attribute (compassion, beauty, wisdom). In the most sophisticated religions individual gods were subservient to, or components of, an ultimate higher reality variously symbolized as a sun or sky god or as infinite potential or emptiness.

This is not to reduce the gods to mere figments of our fertile imagination. Arguably, the power that created and sustained the universe reveals itself to humanity in symbolic forms adjusted to our ability to comprehend. The gods are therefore a synthesis of divine energy and the limitations of human thought.

SATURN
Saturn was the Roman god of seed, agriculture and plenty. His festival, Saturnalia, a celebration of the winter solstice, was a time of freedom and indulgence, and is thought to be the origin of the Christmas celebrations.

TETRA-GRAMMATON
"Four letters", the sacred, unutterable name of God revealed to Moses as the four Hebrew letters YHWH.

Gods and Goddesses

GUANYIN
The Chinese goddess of mercy, a form of the bodhisattva Avalokiteshvara. The thousand-armed bodhisattva who represents infinite compassion.

DURGA
The consort of Shiva is the divine mother of the universe, the destroyer of evil (in which role she is sometimes identified with the terrifying Kali), and the symbol of insight, discrimination, devotion and bliss.

225

SHIVA

One of the great Hindu gods (right), lord of the cosmic dance of destruction followed by renewal. Shiva bears the fire that destroys and the rattle whose sound calls forth creation.

Gods and Goddesses

QUETZAL-COATL

The Plumed Serpent, the Aztec supreme god of the wind and the west (left). Quetzal-coatl was a symbol of wisdom and law-making, and he was responsible for conquering the devouring earth-serpent and rendering the world habitable.

227

WITCHES, PRIESTS AND WIZARDS

Witches, Priests and Wizards

Respected or reviled, those people privy to the inner secrets of true wisdom have always held a special place in society. The idea of witchcraft in the negative sense of "black magic" is ancient and widespread and is thought by anthropologists to have a well-defined social purpose. The evil witch is in fact a scapegoat upon whom calamities and social conflicts can be blamed. Christianity saw witches as the devil's instruments, and the biblical command not to "permit a sorceress to live" was being taken literally as late as 1692, when nineteen women were hanged as witches in

WIZARD
Wizards symbolize magical powers for good (wizards of the right-hand path) or ill (left-hand path), but can also represent the wisdom that comes with age, and the solitary, scholarly life.

Salem, Massachusetts. Female witches were often characterized as seductresses or cannibals, or depicted as owls, cats and toads, all creatures of the night.

The priest has usually symbolized the authorized use of inner wisdom, communicating with higher powers for the benefit of the community. In ancient Egypt and some South American cultures, the rulers were also supreme priests, occupying their temporal position by virtue of their spiritual powers. In few cultures was the priesthood exclusively male.

Wizards, like witches, are capable of serving either good or evil. Essentially workers of ritual magic, in their most exalted form they sought communion with the divine and power to control the forces of nature.

WICKED WITCH Symbolizing destruction and dark powers, the evil witch is usually female. In the West she is often a wizened hag but in Africa she is fat from eating human flesh and red-eyed from nocturnal pursuits.

Witches, Priests and Wizards

HEAVEN AND HELL

Heaven and Hell

For the ancients, the sky was the natural abode of the gods, who controlled sunlight, rain and the other natural forces upon which life depended. Often the gods were believed to live on a solid dome (or firmament) above the earth, from which they observed and judged the activities of mortals. The heavens, or heaven, were thus the obvious place of reward for a good life. And as the opposite of heaven, hell – a dark subter-

PARADISE
In the biblical tradition Paradise (from a Persian word for "garden"), is seen as a place of peace, light, and primordial perfection. The bliss of the first Paradise, Eden, will be restored to the faithful in the form of heaven.

ranean world – came to symbolize the place of punishment and retribution.

Christian artists often depict heaven as a beautiful garden or orchard, while the Norse warriors' heaven of Valhalla was a hall of constant feasting. Visions of hell are similarly diverse. The Christian hell was the fiery abode of the Devil where dire retribution was visited on sinners. In Islamic tradition, the bodies of sinners are enlarged in order to aggravate their suffering in hell. The ancient Greeks believed that Hades consisted of three regions: the Plain of Asphodel, a bleak land where souls wandered aimlessly; the Elysian Fields, the destination of the fortunate few; and Tartarus, where the wicked were punished. Indic religions generally put more emphasis on rebirth and the cycle of existence. For example, in some Buddhist traditions hell is not a final destination but a place where one suffers in order to work off bad *karma* before being reincarnated.

Heaven and Hell

TSHITIGARBHA
The concept of eternal hell is at odds with Buddhist teachings. In Tibetan Buddhism, enduring love and compassion are embodied in the bodhisattva Tshitigarbha, who descends into hell in order to help those suffering there.

Heaven and Hell

JACOB'S LADDER
In the Bible, Jacob dreams of angels ascending and descending steps linking heaven and earth. It symbolizes our yearning for higher consciousness.

FIERY SWORD
The sword that barred Adam and Eve from Eden symbolizes the loss of paradise when we separate ourselves from the divine.

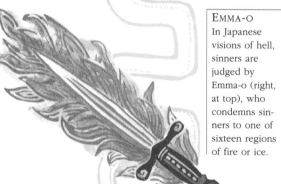

EMMA-O
In Japanese visions of hell, sinners are judged by Emma-o (right, at top), who condemns sinners to one of sixteen regions of fire or ice.

Heaven and Hell

NIRVANA

The supreme goal of Buddhists, Nirvana is beyond description: it is ultimate tranquillity, the release from all the limitations of existence, and is symbolized in only the most abstract form.

FERRYMAN OF THE DEAD

Death has always been symbolized as a journey. For the ancient Greeks, the dead journeyed across the river Styx, ferried by the ghostly boatman Charon.

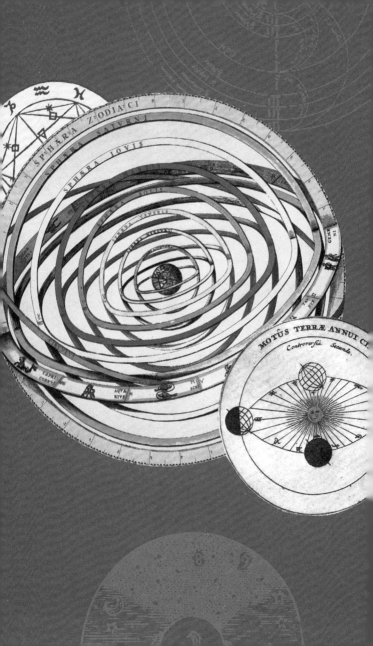

SYMBOL SYSTEMS

 In the extraordinary richness and complexity of symbol systems such as the Tarot, astrology and the Kabbalah, we see human creativity at full stretch. However, the deeper fascination of such systems is that they resonate with fundamental aspects of our own nature, speaking of shared wisdom whose truths we recognize but can never quite put into words.

A symbol system is nothing less than a symbolic map of reality. It represents the topography of the mental and emotional realm that reveals itself to the inner eye. And just as a city cannot be properly appreciated unless we allow ourselves the time and space to study it in every detail, so too a symbol system can only reveal its full meaning if we acquaint ourselves with all its aspects. Like the notes in a symphony, each symbol in the system has meaning not only in its own right, but also in relationship to the other symbols. The whole is much more than the sum of its parts. The mystic and philosopher George Ivanovitch

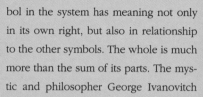

Gurdjieff (1872–1949) suggested that we are like people living in beautiful houses who never leave the basement: unless we venture to explore areas of the mind that lie outside everyday thinking we

remain largely strangers to ourselves. The careful study of a symbol system can lead us to a better knowledge and understanding of our own minds and enable us to live more fully within them.

Those wishing to orientate themselves on the spiritual map that a

symbol system provides usually find that one system
exerts a greater pull than the
rest. In part, this is the result of cultural
factors, but individual temperament also
plays a role. To someone who is artistic,
or has a highly developed visual sense,
a system that uses pictures (such as the
Tarot) may offer the most appeal. A person for whom the body is paramount
over the intellect may lean more toward
a system focused upon the body's
energy centres (such as yoga).

In addition, certain symbol systems
make greater demands on their students
than others. For example, initiation into
some of the occult systems is a lengthy
process, in which the inner truths that
magical symbols represent are revealed
piecemeal, to protect the student from
the psychological damage that a sudden
release of psychic energy could cause.
Similarly, alchemical symbols are deliberately cryptic in order to test the resolve
and motivation of the seeker.

A New Synthesis

All the great symbol systems attempt to reflect paradoxical truths about ultimate reality in a specialized idiom of their own, shifting from common language to aid the shift from common thinking that is required to gain access to the deepest realities. Rational logic, similarly, is incapable of unveiling for us the most important kinds of knowledge. In the modern age, we must learn to recapture instinctive, pre-scientific truths – the ancient beliefs that spiritual symbol systems have handed on to us.

Patient study of a chosen system will refresh our minds not least by suggesting an alternative way of looking at the world. Of course, it would be folly to turn our back on the discoveries of science. But science is now becoming less certain of itself, and with the development of fields such as quantum mechanics we are beginning to regain the old sense of mystery. Einstein, who astounded us by insisting that space is curved, and proved it, now seems perfectly orthodox, even quaint, to those versed in the modern mysteries of science.

The world is moving toward a synthesis of disciplines, one science informing another until the traditional distinctions of knowledge dissolve. We must hope that past and present wisdom, material and spiritual disciplines, will support each other in the same way, the past throwing a deep-reaching spiritual light upon the present – as it does already for many of those who have unravelled the complexities of traditional symbolism and deciphered the hidden meanings contained therein.

KRISHNA AS MACROCOSM
Depictions of Man as macrocosm occur in many symbol systems. In this Indian painting, Krishna, the best-loved of Vishnu's avatars, is shown as a symbol of the world, containing men, animals and the heavens in his body. Four-armed Krishna holds his attributes – the discus, conch, lotus flower and club.

Occult Systems

Occult Systems

The word "occult" means simply "hidden" and an occult system is a system of wisdom which its practitioners feel must be kept secret. The many different systems are united by their use of symbolic devices to effect a change in consciousness that allows adepts to gain insights into their own nature and reality itself.

Western occultism can trace its origins to the *Hermetica* (1st–3rd centuries CE), writings that take the form of dialogues between deities, in which the Greek god Hermes Trismegistus features prominently. They enshrine a number of concepts that emerge later in the history of the occult, such as the duality of matter

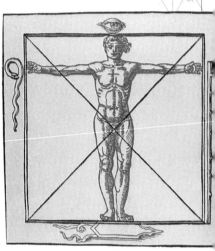

MAGICAL MAN
A 16th-century diagram of Man surrounded by magical symbols.

and spirit, and the idea that salvation can be achieved through knowledge rather than faith. The *Hermetica* views us as immortal spirits trapped in mortal bodies, from which we can achieve liberation, and union with God, by understanding God's true nature.

DEE'S SIGILS
Magical symbols (sigils) devised by the mathematician and occultist Dr John Dee, astrologer at the court of Queen Elizabeth I.

The *grimoires*, magical "recipe books" of the Middle Ages (the most famous being the *Key of Solomon*), set out a system in which self-knowledge,

Occult Systems

and therefore full spiritual evolution, may be attained by the use of symbols to invoke spirits. Having drawn on the ground a complex symbol representing his body, mind and soul, and alongside it a second

triangular shape, the magician summoned the spirit into the triangle and confronted it: if he failed to subdue it, the spirit would enter the first symbol and destroy him. The spirits may be interpreted as facets of the magician's own self, which must be conquered and understood in order to develop a fully integrated personality.

Later occult systems, such as the Hermetic Order of the Golden Dawn (founded in London in 1887), were

ROSY CROSS
Said to have been founded in the 15th century, the mystical fraternity called Order of the Rosy Cross (Rosicrucianism) first became known in 17th-century Germany. Its practices and beliefs drew on alchemy and the Kabbalah.

Occult Systems

strongly influenced by the theories of Eliphas Lévi (see below). In common with many other systems, there were seven levels of initiation. At the highest level, the adept had three tasks: divination, evocation and invocation. In each of these tasks, symbolism played an essential part. When practising evocation, for example, the adept would surround himself with symbols of the god or the part of his own consciousness with which he wished to make contact.

ELIPHAS LÉVI
Adolphe Louis Constant, alias Eliphas Lévi (1810–75), was one of the most influential theoreticians of the occult. This engraving from Lévi's *Transcendental Magic* (right) shows the magician's tools: lamp, rod, dagger and sword.

ALCHEMY

Alchemy is commonly viewed as a pseudo-science concerned with the transformation of base metals into gold: a curiosity, of value mainly for the contributions it made to the emerging science of chemistry. This misconception is understandable given the shroud of secrecy deliberately drawn over the true goal of the alchemists – enlightenment. The symbolism of alchemical transformation was used to disguise what the medieval

MOUNTAIN
A symbolic depiction of the Great Work; at its peak, a pearl represents the rainbow colours (see page 249).

Alchemy

Church condemned as a heretical practice, since it was based upon the belief that the individual could raise himself or herself toward salvation without the agency of established religion.

At the most esoteric level, alchemists aimed to transmute the "base metal" of our everyday thought and experience into the "gold" of a pure, spiritual state. To do this, they sought to discover the Philosopher's Stone, also known as the Elixir or Tincture. Turning base metals into gold was proof of its power, but the elixir was an aim in itself, an essence rather than merely an agent. The journey to enlightenment – known as the Great Work – had interdependent physical and spiritual dimensions.

Alchemy is thought to have originated in ancient Egypt and to have been part of the esoteric wisdom of the Greeks, Arabs, Indians and Chinese. The first alchemical text to appear in western Europe was a 12th-century translation into Latin of the

Alchemy

Alchemy

Arabic *Book of the Composition of Alchemy*. Despite the obscure language of medieval alchemical works, it is clear that the alchemist begins the Great Work with the primal element known as the *materia prima* ("first matter") which one must mine for oneself and takes the form of a "stone" (not to be confused with the Philosopher's Stone). This stone, whose exact nature is not revealed, is pulverized and mixed with a "first agent", placed in a sealed vessel or "philosopher's egg" and heated over a long period. During incubation, the two principles within the *materia prima*, referred to symbolically as "sulphur" (red, male, solar, hot energy) and "mercury" (white,

SYMBOLS OF THE PROCESS
This 17th-century engraving contains symbols of stages in the Great Work. The sun and moon are the male and female elements respectively; the

248

two roses symbolize the Red King and White Queen. Between them is the symbol of mercury, the transforming agent. The lion and snake symbolize raw, unrefined matter.

female, lunar, cold energy) are said to fight and kill each other, producing a black putrefaction, *nigredo*. This ends the first stage of the Great Work.

In the second stage the blackness is overlaid with rainbow colours which are in turn covered by a whiteness, *albedo*. The two principles of the *materia prima* then reappear as the Red King ("sulphur of the wise") emerging from the womb of the White Queen (mercury, or the White Rose). They unite in the fire of love and from their union comes perfection, the Philosopher's Stone: the catalyst for turning base metals into gold and the key to enlightenment.

Correct motivation was essential in

Alchemy

Alchemy

undertaking the Great Work. A seeker driven by greed for gold would, as one alchemical text puts it, "reap but smoke". Instead, one should be motivated "to know nature and its operations, and make use of this knowledge ... to reach the Creator".

The original "stone" that the seeker must mine symbolizes the deep inner longing to find our true spiritual nature, known to alchemists as the "active principle". The "first agent" stands for the "passive principle", the indwelling energy of which most of us are unaware, but which carries the potential for spiritual growth. Once contact is made between the active and passive

PHILOSOPHER'S STONE
This 17th-century alchemical illustration shows the Philosopher's Stone in the furnace (below), and personified as Mercury in the hands of angels (above) The image emphasizes the fact that alchemy is primarily a spiritual quest.

LION EATING THE SUN
In alchemical symbology the green lion (primordial matter), can be said to be either devouring the male principle or liberating the sulphur of the wise (both of which may be symbolized by the sun).

Alchemy

principles within the "furnace" of deep meditation, a struggle ensues as the active principle, used to obtaining what it wants through the exercise of the will, finds that the passive principle cannot be vanquished in this way. There follows the "dark night of the soul", in which both active and passive principles seem to have been annihilated and the individual feels utterly forsaken. However, out of this despair arises the revelation (rainbow) that love and not force is required, and this is followed by the union of the two principles, the Red King and the White Queen, whose progeny is born of water and the spirit.

As for the actual spiritual practices behind this symbolic process, meditating upon the relevant alchemical symbols was certainly involved. A Chinese alchemical text, *The Secret of the Golden Flower*, may give us further clues. It tells us how, through meditation, physical energy can be visualized as concentrating in the lower body in the "place of

ANDROGYNE
The primal elements of sulphur (that which burns) and mercury (that which is volatile) are embodied in the androgyne or hermaphrodite. The union of these opposite principles is the purpose of alchemy and of human endeavour itself. The androgyne wears the crown of perfection and stands on a four-headed dragon, symbolizing its dominion over the elements.

power" below the navel, where it generates great heat and then symbolically passes "the boiling point [and] rises like flying snow ... to the summit of the Creative".

For all their obscure language, perhaps a few alchemists succeeded, effecting the union of the Red King and White Queen to raise the base metal of their physical being into the pure gold of the greater spiritual self.

ALCHEMY AND CHRISTIANITY
Many alchemists were Christians who sought knowledge through experience as well as faith. This image is a later copy of one by a 15th-century English churchman, Sir George Ripley.

THE KABBALAH

The Kabbalah is an extraordinary system of theoretical and practical wisdom designed to provide its students not only with a path of mental and spiritual growth, but also with a symbolic map of creation itself. Rooted in 3rd-century CE Jewish mysticism, the Kabbalah developed in an essentially Hebrew tradition, and the earliest known Kabbalistic text, the *Sefer Yetzira*, appeared some time between the 3rd and 6th centuries. The powerful appeal of the system led to its incorporation into certain aspects of Christian thinking in the 15th century.

Essentially, the Kabbalah is an esoteric teaching centred on a system of symbols that are held to reflect the mystery of God and the universe, and for which the Kabbalist must find the key. At the theoretical level, these keys allow him – the Kaballist has traditionally been male – to understand the spiritual dimensions of the universe, while at the

The Kabbalah

GOD THE
CREATOR
A Christian Kab-
balistic image
of God setting
out the laws
that govern the
universe.

practical level they allow him to use the
powers associated with these dimensions for magical purposes (that is for
the processes of physical, psychological
or spiritual transformation). The keys to
the Kabbalah lie hidden in the meaning

of the divine revelations which make up Holy Scripture. The secrets of Scripture may be revealed through gematria, in which each letter of the Hebrew alphabet has a number associated with it. For example, the brass serpent constructed by Moses to cure snake bite (Numbers 21.9) is converted through gematria to the number 358. This is also the numerical equivalent of the word "Messiah", so the brass serpent is held to be a prophecy of the coming of the Messiah, who will save all those bitten by the longing for truth. Christian Kabbalists adopted the symbol of a serpent draped over the cross to represent Christ.

As well as an understanding of Hebrew, Kabbalists in the past insisted on a number of further stringent conditions before accepting students: a morally pure life; great powers of concentration; and complete dedication to the task. For this reason, the Kabbalah is known to most people only in its most accessible form: the Sefiroth, or Tree of

The Kabbalah

The Kabbalah

Life (opposite). Despite its apparent simplicity, the Sefiroth is itself a powerful and all-encompassing symbol. In its fundamental interpretation, the Sefiroth explains creation. In the act of calling the universe into being, God revealed ten of his attributes, each of which is represented by a symbol called a *sefirah* (plural *sefiroth*, hence the name of the tree). The *sefiroth* are linked together in a set of precise relationships: the path begins at Keter (the Crown) which denotes all that was, is and will be, and leads eventually to Malkhut (the Kingdom) which corresponds to the presence of God in matter. The path leads through the attributes of wisdom, understanding, mercy, judgment, beauty, eternity, reverberation and foundation, and is governed by the three divine principles of Will, Mercy and Justice. In most visualizations of the *sefiroth*, the path takes the form of a zigzag or lightning flash as the divine principles, which are associated with balance (Will),

TREE OF LIFE
The diagram of the Sefiroth was first published in the Middle Ages, and there have since been many variations on its basic struture. In this 20th-century occult version, the ten *sefiroth* are linked by twenty-two paths (the number of letters in the Hebrew alphabet). Superimposed on this version is the great serpent, linked with the Indic *chakra* system of energy centres.

The Kabbalah

expansion (Mercy) and constraint (Justice), operate in turn. The patterns and relationships enshrined in the Sefiroth are fundamental to being and can be applied to all areas of knowledge and endeavour – from cosmic forces to human relationships, from the ascent of the soul to God to the fate of world economies.

In order to account for the many manifestations of God, the Kabbalah contains the concept of the Four Worlds – Manifestation, Creation, Formation and Action – which can be seen as the different aspects of God through which the universe was brought into being. The Four Worlds are usually depicted as four interlocking Sefiroths.

The Kabbalah is essentially an oral tradition and the initiate is usually guided by an experienced mentor. He starts by studying the ten *sefiroth*, ascending the Tree towards full enlightenment. Each *sefirah* represents an aspect of the self that must be fully

GOD'S IMAGE
In Kabbalistic belief, primordial Man, Adam Kadmon, was called forth in the form of the Sefiroth (opposite). Endowed with will, intellect, emotion and a capacity to be conscious of his creator, Adam Kadmon was a reflection of God and an expression of the divine attributes.

developed before the student can proceed to the next stage. For example, he must come to terms with Malkhut, the world of the body and its energies, before he can properly advance to Yesod, the link between body and mind.

Having acquired a theoretical understanding of the ten *sefiroth*, the Kabbalist, through further study and meditation, is able to begin in earnest his ascent through the Tree. Few reach the top of it, but once in Malkhut one can know God and move beyond symbolism to experience infinity itself.

The Kabbalah

COSMIC HOUSE AND MAN

This print (1721) applies the Sefiroth system to a house and the human anatomy.

The Kabbalah

ASTROLOGY

Humankind has always been fascinated by the stars. The ancients were intrigued by the motions and configurations of heavenly bodies, associating them with the mystic powers that governed human fate. In modern astronomy, the old deterministic views of the universe are falling into disfavour, but our awe of the cosmos remains undiminished.

In the earliest communities celestial phenomena were of great practical significance.

ZODIAC SIGNS
The twelve signs of the zodiac are shown in this translation (1489) of an Arabic text.

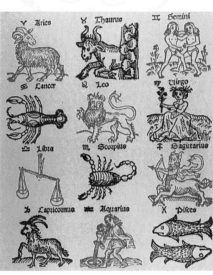

Seasons were measured by the succession of longest and shortest days and the

Astrology

Astrology

times of year when day and night were of equal length. This simple calendar became the basis of planting and hunting. As increasingly detailed celestial records were kept, stars were grouped together into constellations, and the movements of the heavenly bodies were monitored. In time, the constellations became associated with particular objects, animals and mythical figures, and human and divine qualities were projected onto the motions of sun, moon and planets. The skies came alive with imagery of gods, creatures and heroes, and a host of stories relating to this imagery was handed down through the generations. These tales gradually acquired deep mystical significance in explaining humankind's fate, and later still in analyzing human character.

These connections between earth and universe become more credible when we remember that the ancients saw creation as a vast web of interconnected forces. Nothing was uninflu-

ZODIAC MAN
In the idealized microcosmic body of celestial Man (right, from a 15th-century French manuscript), each zodiac sign was associated with a bodily function. Celestial events, such as the position of a planet in a sign, were mirrored in a person's physical and mental well-being.

Astrology

PLANETARY INFLUENCE
This 16th-century English almanac shows the planet Mercury (left). It was seen as a male planet, influencing communication (Mercury was the messenger of the gods). People born under Mercury were held to be alert, fluent, quick-witted and with scientific leanings.

enced by what took place around it, no matter how great the distances concerned. The entrails of a sacrificial animal could indicate the outcome of a battle taking place in a far country; the future was foreseen in dreams; and a handful of stones cast on the ground could guide a person's actions. Human lives were a reflection of the realities written in the heavens.

Astrology – the divinatory system based on the interpretation of stellar and planetary configurations – had its earliest roots in Babylonian civilization. Tablets dating to the 7th century BCE set out the influence on human affairs of four celestial deities: Shamash (the sun),

Sin (the moon), Ishtar (the planet Venus) and Adad (the weather god). Over the centuries, these divinatory principles were transmitted through Egypt, the Near East, India and China, where they developed independently.

However, it was only in the Greco-Roman era that further significant advances were made in the science of astrology. In the 2nd century CE Ptolemy of Alexandria gave the constellations their familiar names. Improved methods of observation then allowed Greek scholars to map the movement of the planets relative to fixed coordinates in the celestial sphere (the visible heavens), rather than to the local sphere (the four compass bearings). The constellations thus formed a backdrop against which the apparent motion of the sun moon and planets (five of which were known in ancient times) around the apparently static earth were charted. The sun and planets appeared to move (relative to the stars) within a narrow

Astrology

band of the sky, and this belt was divided into twelve arcs of 30°. Each division, or "house", was named after the most prominent zodiac constellation that fell within it, but over the millennia the constellations have shifted out of their original houses. For example, at New Year the sun no longer appears in Capricorn but in Sagittarius.

THE PLANETARY SYMBOLS

☉	Sun
☽	Moon
☿	Mercury
♀	Venus
♂	Mars
♃	Jupiter
♄	Saturn
♅	Uranus
♆	Neptune
♇	Pluto

SUN AND MOON

The sun and moon count as planets in astrology. The sun symbolizes the true essence of being while the moon (right) represents imagination and reflectiveness. The dark part of the moon, invisible when we see a bright crescent, is a symbol of the unconscious.

Astrology

In the development of astrology, celestial movements were matched with terrestrial cycles, and the zodiac acquired a symbolism relating to the conditions on earth according to the part of the sky in which the sun appeared. For example, at the height of summer, Leo (the lion) signified the sun's fiery heat. Leo is followed by Virgo (the virgin), symbolic of the fresh seed harvested for next year's planting. Libra (the scales) represented the year balanced between summer and winter, around the autumnal equinox, when day and night are of equal length.

Even in Ptolemy's time the Greeks noted that people appeared to fall into

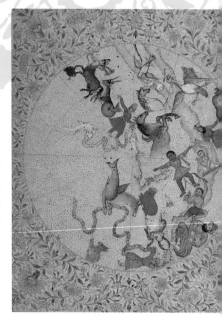

STAR CHARTS
This Moghul Indian illuminated chart of the heavens shows several constellations, including the familiar zodiac

categories of personality according to the season of their birth, and descriptions of twelve personality types gradually evolved that each corresponded approximately to the time when the sun was in one of the signs of the zodiac. From these came the idea of individual horoscopes based on time of birth and various other complex factors. Fatalistic astrology has persisted to this day in more or less the same form.

Astrology

The twelve signs of the zodiac are arranged into four groups of three, and each group is associated with a particular element (fire, water, air or earth) and with a particular quality and gender. The fire signs (Aries, Leo and Sagittarius) are

ones inherited, via the Arabs and Islam, from ancient Hellenistic astrology. The Greek geographer Ptolemy listed 48 constellations.

Astrology

linked to thrusting, energetic characteristics; the water signs (Pisces, Cancer and Scorpio) to emotional and intuitive traits; the air signs (Aquarius, Gemini and Libra) to characteristics of logic and intellect; and the earth signs (Capricorn, Taurus and Virgo) to practicality and dependability. Fire and air signs are, in addition, seen as extroverted, and water and earth signs as introverted.

The influence of the heavenly bodies was thought to depend on the positions of the planets within the signs. Each planet (now ten in all, as the sun and moon are counted as planets for astrological purposes) has a symbol and is said to "rule" one or more of the signs.

The characteristics of each "star sign", the planetary influences and the areas defined by the celestial houses are said to work together to produce a complex web of interrelationships, some complementary, some in opposition, all of which are said to determine the fate of humankind.

Science has denied these connections for centuries and has seen astrology as a pseudo-science, at best a crude forerunner of modern astronomy. Yet the belief that our destiny is in some way bound up with the stars persists. Clearly the symbolic system which astrology represents retains a powerful hold upon our consciousness.

Astrology

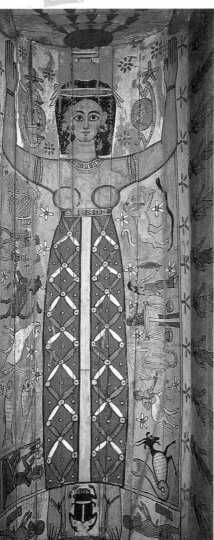

SKY GODDESS
The Egyptian sky goddess Nut, adorned with stars and flanked by zodiac signs, protects the deceased in this 2nd-century CE coffin lid.

273

THE FIRE SIGNS

ARIES

DATES: March 21st–April 19th
SYMBOL: The Ram
RULER: Mars

Aries is fire in its primitive form: impulsive, energetic, dynamic, but potentially uncontrolled and destructive. The energy of Aries needs some outside force to help channel it, and this is provided by Mars, the sign's ruler, which symbolizes our consciousness of our individuality. The ram's qualities are well known: brave and fierce, it puts down its head and charges with great determination at things that arouse it. The rushing ram also represents the first burst of growth in the crops at the onset of spring.

LEO

DATES: July 23rd–August 22nd
SYMBOL: The Lion
RULER: Sun

Leo is fire in its controlled, fixed aspect, burning with a steady glow that illuminates and warms all who come into contact with it. The lion symbolizes life, strength, vigour, regal dignity, pride and courage. It is the

Astrology: The Fire Signs

king of the beasts, ruled by the most powerful of the planets, the sun. Leo denotes a clearer, steadier kind of authority than that of Aries. The lion is one of the most ubiquitous symbols of power, masculinity and leadership. Leo maintains the heat of high summer, ripening the crops for harvest.

SAGITTARIUS

DATES: November 22nd–December 21st
SYMBOL: The Centaur/Archer
RULER: Jupiter

The third of the fire signs possesses the qualities of the other two, but in a more purified and expansive form. Thus Sagittarius has the initiatory power of Aries, but this power is more directed and refined. Like Aries and Leo, Sagittarius is a leadership sign, but is also associated with sensitivity and openness to others' needs and ideas. It marks the transition between autumn and winter.

THE WATER SIGNS

Astrology: The Water Signs

PISCES

DATES: February 20th–March 20th
SYMBOL: Fishes
RULER: Neptune/Jupiter

Deep, mysterious, capable of profound stillness, water symbolizes the energy of the unconscious. The Piscean character is emotional, sensitive, vague and unworldly, given to dreaming and attracted to the unknown. But, like water, the Piscean character is highly fluid and adaptable. Water suggests the Piscean's flow toward others – a gentle, compassionate nature that can show itself as vulnerability. Pisces is a time when late winter and early spring rains prepare the earth for a burst of activity.

CANCER

DATES: June 21st–July 22nd
SYMBOL: The Crab
RULER: The Moon

Cancer is water in its stiller, more controlled aspect. The Cancerian, like the Piscean, is sensitive, affectionate and emotional, but less vulnerable in relationships and more sociable. Ruled by the moon, Cancer has a

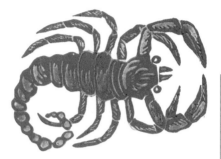

Astrology: The Water Signs

temperamental side. Other qualities are an independent spirit, soundness, calmness, clarity of vision and dependability. Stillness suggests a love of tradition, but the sign (like all water signs) may be strong, imaginative and intuitive. Cancer is the time of the summer solstice, the time of greatest light.

SCORPIO
DATES: October 24th–November 21st
SYMBOL: Scorpion/ Eagle
RULER: Mars/Pluto

The most profound and emotional of signs, Scorpio embodies the calm of all water signs as well as great self-discipline and strength of purpose. Scorpios are intuitive, steadfast, clear-sighted and capable of spiritual transformation and deep understanding – but also of jealousy and possessiveness. They are intense and often withdrawn. During Scorpio, autumn is well established. Animals retreat into regenerating hibernation.

THE AIR SIGNS

AQUARIUS
DATES: January 21st–February 19th
SYMBOL: The Water Carrier
RULER: Saturn/Uranus

Aquarius shows the element air in its freest, most pervasive form. This gives the Aquarian character a sense of universality, which leads to good works and helping others.

In fact, Aquarius is the most humanitarian sign in the zodiac – compassionate and visionary, with a sense of community. Yet there is also a reticence, partly due to Saturn's presence in the sign. Aquarius carries the water of knowledge, symbolizing a desire both to acquire learning and also to share it.

GEMINI
DATES: May 21st–June 20th
SYMBOL: The Heavenly Twins
RULER: Mercury

Whereas Aquarius is air in its searching, pervasive aspect, Gemini is air in its changeable, whimsical, mercurial form. Sometimes referred to as the most child-like sign of the zodiac, Gemini

Astrology: The Air Signs

exhibits a great need to relate to others. The sign symbolizes contradictions, the twins denoting a tendency to go to opposite extremes. The Gemini character, being adaptable, is content with its own paradoxical nature. Like all air signs, Gemini has stronger links with the intellect than with the emotions.

LIBRA
DATES: September 23rd–October 23rd
SYMBOL: The Scales
RULER: Venus

As the symbol suggests, Libra is the sign most associated with justice. The Libran character combines the humanitarianism of Aquarius with the curiosity of Gemini, holding these and other

qualities in a state of balance. Like other air signs, Libra embodies the intellect, but its innate balance prevents the strictly rational approach to life from overwhelming the intuitive. It also represents equilibrium between physicality and spirituality.

THE EARTH SIGNS

CAPRICORN

DATES: December 22nd–January 20th
SYMBOL: The Goat
RULER: Saturn

Capricorn is the essence of earth, associated with stability and structure. The Capricorn character is thus cautious, practical and orderly. The goat is also stubborn or, more positively, deter-mined and self-disciplined. Saturn lends Capricorn a deliber-ate, serious man-ner, a liking for solitude and occasionally a dark, depressive side. Capricorn's mystical side is likely to be expressed as an interest in earth mysteries and nature's hidden forces. In Capri-corn life looks inward in prepa-ration for spring.

TAURUS

DATES: April 20th–May 20th
SYMBOL: The Bull
RULER: Venus

Taurus is earth in its more visi-ble aspect. Like the bull, Taurus is courageous, strong, fiery, dif-ficult and deter-mined, but at other times dependable and capable. Venus as ruler means that the Taurean has a keen eye

Astrology: The Earth Signs

for natural beauty and perhaps a strong sexual motivation. There is a jealous and possessive side too, but also generosity and kindness. With spring at its peak, Taurus represents the full realization of the creative forces of nature.

VIRGO
DATES: August 23rd–September 22nd
SYMBOL: The Virgin
RULER: Mercury

Virgo is the sign of application. It is concerned with how the earth is made and the uses to which it may be put. It stands for transformation, a taking apart of the earth to study its nature, and then moulding it to suit human needs. The Virgo character is analytical and often overly critical. Mercury as ruling planet contributes a restless, nervy tension. But Virgo is also associated with dependability and sincerity. It signifies great activity on land, as people harvest the rewards of their labours.

THE TAROT

The Tarot

The Tarot cards are in effect two packs in one: the *major arcana*, which consist of twenty-two trump cards, each one unique; and the *minor arcana*, which differ from modern playing cards only in that there are four court cards in each suit (king, queen, knight and page or princess) instead of three, and that the suits themselves are pentacles (or coins), cups, wands and swords. It seems likely that the two packs were once separate.

The origins of the Tarot remain a mystery. Attempts have been made to trace it back variously to the ancient civilizations of Egypt, India and China, and its introduction into Europe has been credited to both the Arabs and the Roma (Gypsies). How the two packs became combined into one is also unclear. Recognizing their similar purpose, occultists in northern Italy may have used them as alternatives, with the result that over the years they became more and more

closely associated until the distinction between them disappeared.

During this period the cards went through many modifications. The first recorded pack to resemble the modern Tarot was made for the Duke of Milan in 1415, though seventeen Tarot cards in Paris are claimed by some to come from a deck made for Charles VI of France in 1392. What is certain is that from the early 15th century the cards came to be widely used in France and Italy, and eventually spread throughout Europe. In the course of time their original intention became overlaid by their role as playing cards. The major arcana proved too complex for playing purposes and disappeared from what is now the modern playing pack.

There is a strong tradition that locates

The Tarot

GAME CARDS
Les tarots was the name of a French card game that was the forerunner of bridge. Its Italian equivalent was *tarocchi*. These late 19th-century *tarocchi* cards form part of the major arcana.

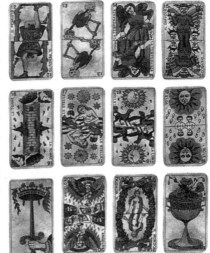

The Tarot

the Tarot's origins in the body of wisdom said to have been laid down by the Egyptian god Thoth (the Greek Hermes Trismegistus) for his disciples in magic. Inspired by this theory, an 18th-century Paris wigmaker and fortune teller who called himself Etteilla (his real name, Alliette, in reverse) devised his own Tarot pack for divination. Eliphas Lévi (see page 245) later extended Etteilla's ideas into a complete system based on Egyptian images but linked also with the Kabbalah. Lévi's interpretation is based on suspect premises, but the Kabbalistic echoes of the Tarot are undeniable. For example, the twenty-two letters of the Hebrew alphabet correspond with the twenty-two major arcana; and the four suits of the minor arcana could be said to reflect the four Kabbalistic Four Worlds (see page

WAITE PACK
The Waite pack (below) in many ways revolutionized the Tarot in the 20th century. Designed by Arthur Edward Waite, a member of the Hermetic Order of the Golden Dawn (see page 244), and painted by Pamela Colman, the Waite (or

"Rider") pack inspired many later packs and is popular worldwide. The minor arcana cards show scenes rather than merely the number of symbols from the suit, and this extends the scope of the diviner's interpretation of the images.

260). Lévi's theories were a significant influence on Arthur Edward Waite (see left), who devised one of the most popular packs in use today.

The major arcana constitute one of the most intriguing of all symbol systems, combining mysteries of the past with a complex and powerful system of inner growth. To spend time with the Tarot and identify with its images is to commence a journey of self-discovery that can leave the individual profoundly changed. The twenty-two cards that make up the major arcana are a symbolic synopsis of our own nature. One way of expressing this is that they are an attempt to represent the factors that constitute our personality – an attempt that pre-dates the efforts of modern psychologists by more than five hundred years.

The Tarot

JUDGEMENT.

★ WORKING WITH THE TAROT

In order to make use of the major arcana as a method of self-discovery, it is necessary to spend time reflecting on what each of the twenty-two cards represents. Read the descriptions given in the following pages, then take one card at a time, and for several days allow your mind to return to it as often as you can. Put the card somewhere prominent and look at it as often as possible. Allow the image to become fixed in your mind, so that you are able to visualize it in detail. Ask the card's central image what it has to tell you about yourself.

Don't worry whether you are talking to an image that has objective reality or simply to an aspect of your own unconscious. In all work with symbols, results come only if we cease to plague ourselves with the need for logical explanations. The image is simply there, existing in its own dimension. Let it do the work

for you. In this way, use each of the twenty-two cards in turn in the order in which they appear in the pack, from The Fool to The World. Don't allow personal preferences for certain cards to influence you unduly. Don't regard some cards as "good" and others as "bad". Each has its part to play.

After a time each card will start to stimulate self-insights. Some of these will be aspects of yourself that are already well known and accepted by you. Others will be more shadowy – this is an important discovery in itself. When you feel that a card has revealed all it can for now, move on, but don't rush things.

Draw or paint the card to help it speak directly to your unconscious. Once you can visualize it clearly with eyes closed, sit in a relaxed but upright position and meditate deeply upon it by holding it in your awareness and disregarding any extraneous thoughts. Next, imagine that the frame around the image

Working with the Tarot

Working with the Tarot

is the frame of a door, and that you are looking out onto the scene in front of you. Then step through the door and become part of the scene. Notice how at this point events may take on a life of their own, as in a dream. Allow the scene to unfold and see what happens.

When you have worked through all twenty-two cards, you will have a deeper and richer awareness of aspects of yourself. Analyze this awareness. Are some aspects of yourself clearly undeveloped and needing more freedom? Do other aspects arouse shame? Are other aspects obvious strengths, which can be allowed more space to flourish?

You may notice, as you proceed through the cards, a cumulative effect of insights from the earlier cards being carried into your work with the later ones. The order in which you face them is important. You cannot proceed properly to The Magician, until you have recognized in yourself the innocence represented by The Fool. You cannot proceed to The High Priestess, until you have recognized The Magician within yourself, your own inner power to change.

For many people, the best-known use of the major arcana (some systems employ the minor as well) is as a means of divination, to reveal certain things about the personality or to provide advice about problems or insights into the future. It is well to remember that occult tradition claims other, superior purposes for the Tarot. In divination each card is interpreted by a diviner, instead of revealing itself more fully through meditation and study. At the end of each of the descriptions that follow are some of the divinatory meanings usually attached to each card, but if you wish to use the pack for this purpose you should first go through the process described above, so that each card is allowed to come properly alive for you. In any case, it goes without saying that divination is best done for yourself, rather than by another person.

Working with the Tarot

FRANCE J IERGER

LE·FOU

0. FOOL

In the medieval world the fool or jester was seen as possessing a naive wisdom that made him wiser at times than those around him. In the Tarot, The Fool is that part of ourselves that is wise enough to stand awestruck before the mystery of creation, and bold enough to set off exploring. The Fool is the only card in the major arcana that is unnumbered, and he has no set position in the order of the cards. Carrying the minimum of possessions and the pilgrim's staff, egged on by a strange animal (sometimes a cat or dog) symbolizing the inner motivation that snaps at our heels once we start to question the nature of reality, The Fool steps toward the unknown – the inner self. *Divinatory meaning*: Unplanned incident or endeavour; unexpected new beginning. Can turn out well if flanked by fortunate cards, otherwise can indicate an unwise move. *Reversed*: impetuous foolishness.

I. MAGICIAN

The Magician (or Juggler) is the part of ourselves that inaugurates self-transformation. Without some inner magic, our real self will lie forever hidden under the confused world of emotions, physical needs and conditioning. In some packs, the implements on the table in front of him are the pentacle, chalice, wand and sword, symbolizing respectively existence, love, wisdom and inner realization, and also the four elements. *Divinatory meaning*: Foreseen or planned new beginning; self-confidence, strength of will, readiness to take risks. *Reversed*: Weak will, inability to grasp opportunities.

The Tarot: The Major Arcana

The Tarot: The Major Arcana

LA PAPESSA

II. HIGH PRIESTESS

The High Priestess embodies the hidden, mystic, receptive feminine principle that awaits the energy of the overt, active, male principle. We can only undertake the developmental journey of the major arcana by acknowledging what the high priestess symbolizes within ourselves. Enigmatic and beautiful, she holds the book of wisdom. She is the oracle and knows the answers to all questions. *Divinatory meaning*: Intuitive insight, creative ability, revelation of hidden things. *Reversed*: Emotional instability, lack of insight, enslavement to a woman.

III. EMPRESS

The Empress is the bringer of maternal fertility, the earth-mother presiding over the creation and destiny of sons and daughters. She wears a diadem representing the gifts we receive at birth, and on her shield is an eagle, a symbol of heaven, the sun and a host of positive attributes including courage and clear vision. She represents the conscious mind and unites matter and spirit. *Divinatory meaning*: Fertility, growth, strength from nature, comfort and security. *Reversed*: impoverishment, stagnation, domestic upheaval.

L'IMPERATRIS

IIII. EMPEROR

The Emperor is the archetype of male power – of strength, leadership, achievement. He holds a royal orb and sceptre, which denote his power to guide the world and are also phallic symbols of male energy. Within the material world over which he rules there is the hidden spiritual world, which is attainable only when the male is united with the female. Empress and Emperor combine complementary aspects of a divine unity. *Divinatory meaning*: Vigour, self-control, ambition, leadership, strength. *Reversed*: Failure of ambition, subservience, loss of influence.

The Tarot: The Major Arcana

V. HIEROPHANT

The Hierophant (priest), sometimes called The Pope, is male energy expressed as spiritual power, the feminine in the male. He is enthroned, like The Emperor, but he rules by faith not force. He wears the red robe of external power, but the blue robe of internal power shows under it. His three-tiered crown and triple cross represent the Trinity and his rule on three planes – physical, intellectual, spiritual. *Divinatory meaning*: Knowledge, wisdom, inspirational help, wise counsel. *Reversed*: Misinformation, slander, bad advice.

The Tarot: The Major Arcana

VI. LOVERS

In many packs this card shows a man flanked by two women, one pure and respectable, the other beautiful and wanton. Above their heads Cupid blindly points his arrow. Having recognized the need for male to unite with female at the level of the inner self, the choice is now between the two archetypes of femininity: the virginal and sacred (The Priestess), and the fertile and material (The Empress). *Divinatory meaning*: Attraction, love, partnership, looming choice. *Reversed*: Indecision, relationship problem, aversion.

VII. CHARIOT

The charioteer (often female in early packs) has something of the androgyne. The breastplate is the armour of maleness, but on the shoulders are feminine lunar symbols. He is bound for the heavens, as emphasized in some packs by stars around his head and wings on the chariot. The Waite pack shows a city in the background, but the charioteer turns his back on such worldliness. *Divinatory meaning*: Deserved success, good progress. *Reversed*: Egocentricity, insensitivity, ruthlessness, progress at others' expense.

VIII. JUSTICE

Justice, traditionally a female figure, shows the assimilation of outer forces by the conqueror. She wears the red robe of worldly power, and holds a sword and pair of scales. In the Tarot the sword symbolizes spiritual realization, not vengeance. Justice uses her power only to cut through those things that impede realization. The scales allow her to weigh the value of all things and to maintain a balance between outer and inner. *Divinatory meaning*: Sound judgment, arbitration, negotiation agreement. *Reversed*: Injustice, prejudice.

The Tarot: The Major Arcana

VIIII. HERMIT

The Hermit represents the loneliness of the spiritual quest. He is elderly and age is a symbol of wisdom, of the realization that comes from experience. He also symbolizes perseverance and the fact that each of us must find enlightenment – our real self, the inner truth – unaided. He holds a lantern, a guiding light, and a pilgrim's staff that is also the wand that drives out ignorance. *Divinatory meaning*: Need for space or solitude, self-sufficiency, self-reliance, discretion, silence. *Reversed*: Rejection of others (or advice), isolationism, obstinacy.

The Tarot: The Major Arcana

X. WHEEL OF FORTUNE

The wheel represents movement. Each time we return to a point we are potentially richer for having experienced the full revolution of the wheel. The wheel may bear a trio of mythical creatures: one descending, representing our instincts; one ascending, representing intelligence, climbing heavenward; and one on top, symbolizing spiritual knowledge. *Divinatory meaning*: Good fortune, major events, big change in life circumstances. *Reversed*: End of a cycle of good fortune.

XI. STRENGTH

Usually shown as a female figure (a male figure in some packs) overcoming an open-mouthed lion. The message is that as well as the physical strength symbolized by the raw energy of the lion, there is a higher, spiritual strength, the awareness of the immortal, indestructible power inside us which transcends materiality and is not affected by its disintegration. *Divinatory meaning*: Well-won triumph over oneself or others, reconciliation, an opportunity seized. *Reversed*: Defeat, surrender to one's baser instincts or to others, a missed opportunity.

XII. HANGED MAN

The man hangs upside down, an old punishment for debtors. The gibbet's uprights and crosspiece represent three, the number of creation, yet the man's legs cross in a four, the number of completion. We must follow our own path from creation to completion, whatever the cost. *Divinatory meaning*: Flexibility, self-sacrifice in a good cause; responsiveness to intuition, losing undesirable qualities. *Reversed*: Failed inner struggle, unresponsiveness to intuition, refusal to shed undesirable qualities.

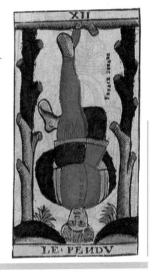

XIII. DEATH

Death appears as a skeleton with a scythe, symbolizing the liberation of the self from the body. The card also bears the number 13. Death, though, is not a final annihilation to be feared but a necessary part of the cycle of existence, thus it is not the last card but a transitional one between the two halves of the pack. In some cultures a symbolic death is part of the initiation into the spiritual world. The card in fact represents spiritual transformation. *Divinatory meaning*: Blessing in disguise, end of negative situation, transforming experience. *Reversed*: Inertia, lethargy, stagnation.

The Tarot: The Major Arcana

XIIII. TEMPERANCE

A symbol of peace and tranquillity. Temperance is shown filling with the waters of new life the empty vessel left by the death of the ego. Losing the ego means stripping ourselves of misconceptions, pride, and the attachments and aversions we show toward the transient experiences of material life. Temperance provides us with the sustenance to go further. *Divinatory meaning*: Skilful combination of circumstances, moderation, circumspection. *Reversed*: Inept combination of circumstances, competing interests, excess.

XV. DEVIL

even after the death of the ego and the sustenance of temperance, there are pitfalls. We still face the underworld, symbolized by The Devil, as well as a higher world. However, the card's message is not one of evil but of trial. The Devil is, as it were, the quality controller, challenging us to look deeper into ourselves, lest we take the path of personal power. *Divinatory meaning*: Challenge, redirection or transformation of physical energy into more mental or spiritual pursuits. *Reversed*: Repression of inner self, lust for material power and gain.

The Tarot: The Major Arcana

XVI. TOWER

Following the challenge set by The Devil, The Tower is struck by lightning (divine justice). This is purifying and beneficial: The Tower (or House of God) symbolizes a casting out of those remaining aspects of the self which are capable of hindering our unity of being. It symbolizes the positive energy that can come from destruction. *Divinatory meaning*: Unexpected challenge, abrupt change in inner life, release of emotions and repressed feelings. *Reversed*: Avoidable calamity, being unbalanced by events, emotional repression.

XVII. STAR

Like Temperance, The Star carries two pitchers, but instead of pouring from one into the other she empties one into a pool of water (the unconscious) and the other onto the ground (the consciousness). The overriding symbolism is that of rebirth: having been purged of remnants of the ego, we now experience rebirth in a higher realm of being. *Divinatory meaning*: Sudden widening of horizons, new life and vigour, deep insight. *Reversed*: Reluctance to take broader view, self-doubt, lack of trust and openness.

The Tarot: The Major Arcana

XVIII. MOON

The Moon is a feminine symbol *par excellence* and we are now poised for the final reconciliation between the opposite poles of our being, male and female, conscious and unconscious, outer and inner. But baying dogs, snapping crayfish and mighty towers symbolize barriers to full understanding. *Divinatory meaning*: Intuition rather than reason; self-reliance. *Reversed*: Failure of nerve, fear of the unknown.

XIX. SUN

The Sun is the root symbol of the male. Here we see The Sun in full splendour, and in many early Tarot packs its radiance falls upon an embracing man and a woman (or Gemini, the Twins). Full union has taken place, two have become one. The sense of alienation, separation and fragmentation at the heart of human unease has disappeared. However, the quester's journey is never-ending. Beyond the level reached in The Sun there are other levels to be traversed, high above human comprehension. For the moment, though, we can savour the triumph of the spirit. *Divinatory meaning*: Achievement, success, triumph over odds, safety after peril, a just reward. *Reversed*: Misjudgment, illusory success, exposure of success obtained by dubious means.

LE JUGEMENT

XX. JUDGMENT
The Judgment shows an angelic figure sounding a trumpet, and a grave opening to release the dead. The card is a representation of the Last Trump, when the human race itself is awakened. The angel represents the next stage in the spiritual journey. Having reached enlightenment, our task is to turn back and rouse our fellows, like the bodhisattva in Buddhism, who, on the threshold of Nirvana, refuses to enter until all of the human race can enter as well. *Divinatory meaning*: Return to health, justified pride in achievement, a new lease of life. *Reversed*: Punishment for failure, regret for lost opportunities.

The Tarot: The Major Arcana

The Tarot: The Major Arcana

XXI. WORLD
Surrounded by a victory wreath, a naked woman holds a taper or a magician's wand. Around the wreath are the four creatures of Ezekiel, symbols of divine truth. The aspirant is now free from the prison of ignorance. Twenty-one is the occult number of completion (three times seven), but the number of absolute unity, infinity, unlimited potential. is zero, the number of The Fool. We have come full circle: we have lost all preconceptions and, like The Fool, see things as they are.

TANTRA

Tantra is a system of occult practices that embraces aspects of Hindu, Buddhist and Jain belief. The practitioner, or *tantrika*, explores each of the energies of his own being, transforming them in the process into the subtler energies of the spirit. Tantra harnesses the exuberant extremes of life, in contrast to the more traditional spiritual path of denial. It accepts that, properly invoked, each of the creative energies within men and women is potentially spiritual energy. Only when each of these energies is acknowledged and allowed to unite with the other elements of the mind can men and women ascend to the ultimate state of being.

The symbols used in Tantra are among the richest contained in any symbol system. The great cosmic diagram of the cult is the Sri Yantra (see page 101), which provides a focus for meditation. However, the most striking Tantric symbols are associated with sexuality. These are frequently taken in the West as evidence of depravity and licentiousness, but in fact they represent the fact that sexual energy can be used

Tantra

by the adept for the purposes of spiritual growth. In Tantra, sexual arousal can be used to hold the adept for long periods in the highest bliss the body can experience. This bliss is not dissipated in orgasm, but retained in the body in a subtler form, which can help the adept climb further up the spiritual ladder.

The *yoni* (vulva) is a recurrent image in Tantric iconography, reflecting the view that the world's existence is a continuous birth. In parallel with this is the notion of continuous and ecstatic fertilization by the male seed. The male organ is represented by the *lingam*, and the female by various vulvic images such as the lotus flower. Creation is expressed in erotic terms as the union of Shiva and Shakti.

Also central to Tantra is the idea of the subtle body, the basis of yogic practice. The adept visualizes the universe encircling the mythical Mount Meru, and then proceeds to identify the spine with the mountain's central axis, so that the

TANTRIC
ICONOGRAPHY
This 18th-century Tibetan *thangka* encapsulates Tantric symbolic art, in which symbolic diagrams based on geometric shapes (and often spiritual figures) are used in meditation. The image includes the mandalas of the Wrathful Buddhas, the Peaceful Buddhas and the Knowledge-Holders.

Tantra

adept becomes cosmic. The adept locates each particular aspect of the world as flowing in a stream from his or her own being, and focuses these streams upon the *chakra*s – energy centres within the subtle body. Hindu Tantra emphasizes the lowest *chakra*, at the base of the spine, where the subtle serpent Kundalini dwells. When awakened by yogic exercise, the serpent activates the energy of the central spine. Kundalini rises to each higher *chakra* in turn until time is transcended and the reality beyond time experienced.

THE *YIJING*

Do we live in a universe in which objects and events are individual and disconnected, or one where everything that happens is part of a single, vast, interrelated whole? If this holistic view is correct, there is in a real sense no such thing as chance. Every happening, even the turn of a card or fall of a coin, is caused by a chain of preceding events, whether these be apparent to the senses or not.

The Chinese *Yijing* (*I Ching*), or *Book of Changes*, one of the oldest methods of divination known to humankind, reflects the philosophy of interconnectedness. Dating back to between 1000BCE and 750BCE, the book has been extensively supplemented by commentaries added by sages thought to include Confucius himself. Briefly, it consists of a set of continuous and broken lines, the former representing "yes" (*yang*) and the latter "no" (*yin*). Each

The Yijing

permutation of three lines (trigram) or six lines (hexagram) is associated with a particular group of meanings. The toss of coins, or the casting of a bunch of yarrow sticks, determines which of these combinations provides the answer to the question.

The *Yijing* symbolizes the universal presence of opposites: night and day, good and evil, fortune and misfortune, and so on. It recognizes that our perception of reality is based on these opposites, but acknowledges that the opposites are mutable and that nothing is permanent. The two opposing trigrams of three continuous lines (Qian) and three broken lines (Kun) progressively take on aspects of each other (see page 311) until the distinction between them disappears.

At some point the eight trigrams were put together to form the sixty-four hexagrams, and these together were thought to represent all the basic human situations. To identify which of the sixty-

The Yijing

four hexagrams provides the answer to a particular question, the quester takes three small coins (easier to come by than yarrow sticks) and tosses them six times in succession. The combination of heads and tails produced each time determines whether to select a continuous or a broken line. Starting from the bottom, the quester records the appropriate line after each throw, eventually ending up with the six lines of a hexagram. The meaning symbolized by the hexagram is then read from the relevant passage in the pages of the *Yijing*.

The 64 hexagrams laid out as a square. The hexagrams of six continuous and six broken lines are in opposite corners.

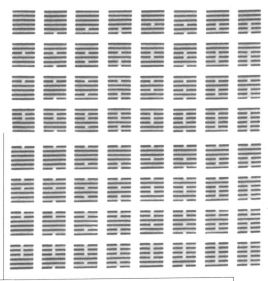

YIJING THEORY Our knowledge of the present is only partial, and in divination we cannot know which parts of the present relate to which parts of the future. We can only symbolize aspects of the present in the form of numbers. Once these numbers are known, future events can be calculated from them according to a set of fixed laws. In the *Yijing* these numbers are revealed by tossing coins, because everything is meaningful in an interconnected universe.

The Yijing

TRIGRAMS
Anyone who wishes to consult the *Yijing* fully needs the 64 hexagrams and their attendant explanations. But working initially with the eight trigrams provides a good introduction to the *Yijing*. The trigrams are given here (right), with their names and meanings. Note that they provide suggestive advice, not instructions. With the trigrams we throw the coins three times only.

 QIAN: The creative; heaven; the father; active.

 KUN: The receptive; earth; mother; passive.

 JIAN: The arousing; movement; peril; thunder.

 KAN: The deep; water; pit; danger.

 GEN: The still; high places; arresting progress.

 XUN: The gentle; wood; wind; penetration.

 LI: The clinging; fire; beauty; brightness.

 DUI: The joyous; pleasure; lake; satisfaction.

The Yijing

GLOSSARY

ALCHEMY A medieval forerunner of chemistry concerned with the transmutation of base metals into gold, but also a symbolic process of spiritual transformation of the self.

AMULET A charm worn or carried to ward off evil.

ARCHETYPES In Jungian theory, universally meaningful symbolic images and ideas that emerge from the collective unconscious. Archetypes transcend time, culture and heredity, although they may vary in detail from one individual to another.

ASTROLOGY A system of DIVINATION based on the interpretation of celestial configurations.

BODHISATTVA In Buddhism, one who attains the state of Nirvana but delays doing so in order to help others less fortunate.

CARDINAL POINTS The four chief points of the compass – north, east, south and west.

CHAKRAS The psychic and spiritual energy centres in the etheric body corresponding to certain organs in the physical body. The *chakras* symbolize spiritual ascent, and form the basis of a system of meditation.

DIVINATION Obtaining knowledge, especially of the future, by occult means.

ETHERIC BODY A subtle body, similar in shape to the physical body, through which life-energy is said to flow. The etheric body interpenetrates every atom of the physical body and is visible to clairvoyants as a network of energy streams.

KARMA In Buddhism and Hinduism, the moral law of cause and effect in which an individual's actions in one life are rewarded or punished in subsequent incarnations.

KABBALAH In the Judaic tradition, a symbolic system of theoretical and practical wisdom providing a means to mental and spiritual growth as well as a symbolic representation of creation. See also *SEFIROTH*.

MACROCOSM The "great world", the wider universe. See also MICROCOSM.

MAJOR ARCANA The twenty-two picture cards in the Tarot pack, which carry allegorical scenes. They are used as a guide on the spiritual journey and in divination.

MANDALA A symbolic diagram based on geometric shapes and often including a human or divine figure, used as a basis of meditation in Eastern mysticism. It is enclosed in a circle and symbolizes the MACROCOSM.

MANTRA In Buddhism and Hinduism, a sacred sound chanted or repeated inwardly during meditation.

MICROCOSM A miniature model of the MACROCOSM. Philosophers saw the human body as a reflection of the universal whole.

MINOR ARCANA The four suits, each of fourteen cards, in the Tarot pack: pentacles (or coins), cups, wands and swords.

NIRVANA In Buddhist philosophy, the ultimate blessed state to which the practitioner aspires, free from the cycle of continual death and rebirth.

OCCULT "Hidden". Term used to describe a system of mystical wisdom kept secret by its practitioners.

PENTAGRAM (or pentacle) A five-pointed star drawn with five continuous strokes used as a sacred or magical symbol.

SEFIRAH (Plural: *sefiroth.*) One of ten aspects of God revealed during the creation of the universe and represented in the Kabbalistic *SEFIROTH*, or Tree of Life.

SEFIROTH The Tree of Life, the most familiar symbol of the Kabbalah. The *sefiroth* graphically sets out the stages of God's manifestation and the relationships that underlie the whole of existence and creation. Each point on the Tree is associated with a *SEFIRAH*, whence the name.

SHAMAN In many cultures, a priest-like figure who communicates with the spirit world.

SYMBOL SYSTEM A symbolic "map" of reality that represents the fundamental aspects of our emotional and spiritual experience and can be used as a means of exploring and developing the spiritual self.

TALISMAN An object, often a representation of a god or goddess, that is supposed to be invested with the powers of the deity in question.

TANTRA An Indian cult in which the practitioner explores the energies (often sexual) of his or her own being and transforms them into subtler, spiritual energies.

TAROT A card pack used for spiritual growth and divination. See also MAJOR ARCANA and MINOR ARCANA.

YANTRA A symbolic geometric diagram used as a basis of meditation in Eastern mysticism.

YIJING (I CHING) A Chinese system of divination in which the practitioner interprets linear patterns derived by casting yarrow sticks or coins.

YIN AND YANG In Chinese philosophy, the two opposing but complementary principles determining the destiny and structure of the universe. *Yin* is feminine, negative and dark; *yang* is masculine, positive and light.

ZODIAC The band in the sky through which the sun, moon and planets appear to move, and in which the 12 zodiacal constellations are located.

Glossary

INDEX

Index

Page numbers in *italic* type refer to captions.

Adam and Eve *232*
Adam Kadmon *260*
Aeolus *182*
agate *199*
ages of man 211
Agni *184*
Ahura Mazda *197*
air *92*, *97*, 180, 182–183
   astrological signs 272,
   278–279
alchemy *13*, 46, *49*,
   144, 180, 246–254
amulet 111
androgyne 50, *252*
angel *217*
anima/animus (arche
   types) 20–21, *20*, *21*
   49 see also male and
   female
animals 32–37, 39,
   129–163
ankh *95*
Anubis *140*
Aphrodite 57, *179*
apocalypse *121*
Apollo 57, *122*, 168
apple *179*, *213*
Aquarius 278
archer 275
architecture 126–128
Aries (astrology) 274
armour 294
arrow *121*, *214*
Artemis 57, 151, *154*,
   208 see also Diana
Asphodel, Plain of 231
aspen 168
astrology 263–281
star charts 270–271 *see*
   also star

Aurora *203*
Avalokiteshvara *101*, *225*

Ba *145*
Babylon *152*
Bacchus 56 *see also*
   Dionysus
baptismal font 114
basilisk *161*
Bastet *141*
bat *158*
bear *154*
Beelzebub 157
beetle *26*
Bellerophon *183*
belly 25
Big Dipper *202*
bird 143–145, 166
birth of Venus *146*
black 108, *110*, 249
   agate *199*, horse *137*
Blake, William 55
blood of Christ *45*
blue *109*, robe 293
boar *156*
boat *188*
Bodhidharma *188*
bodhisattvas 27, 100,
   101, *225*, *231* 301
body *96*, 173, *180*,
   212–215
Book of the Dead,
   Egyptian 42
Botticelli, Sandro *146*
bow and arrow *121*
Brahma *69*, 146, 196
bread *45*, 176
bridge *128*
bull 153, 280, and
   Europa *154*
butterfly *131*

caduceus *136*, *151*
Cancer (astrology) *148*,
   276–277
Canis Major *140*
Capricorn 280
castle *127*
cat *110*, *142*, 229
cave 33, *191*, paintings
   32, 33
Celtic cross *95*, triple
   enclosure *98*
centaur *163*, 275
Ceres 155
*chakra*s 206, *258*, 306
chalice 45, 291
chariot *42*, *119*, 294
Charon 58, *234*
chimera 159, *161*
Chiron *163*
Christ 45, *45*, *104*, *108*,
   112, *179*, *200*, 211, 257
Christmas tree *168*
chrysanthemum *164*
church 126
circle 53, *91*, *92*, *95*,
   96, *136*, stone *127*
city 294
clock maze *103*
clothes *211*
cloud *189*
coat of arms *116*
cockerel 131, *138*
collective unconscious
   13, 14, 38–39, 44, 73, 77
colour 87–89, 108–110,
   248–249
comet *203*
conch *148*
cord 124, *125*
corn *117*
corn doll *209*
cornucopia *209*
cosmic man *96*
cosmos 89, *91*

cow 22
crab 276
craftsmen, rituals of 112
crayfish 300
creation myth 41, 206
crescent 91, 204
crest 116
crocodile 56
Cronos 22, 155, 212
cross 85–86, 88, 177,
    214, Celtic 95,
    inverted 95, rosy 71,
    95, 244, swastika 95,
    triple 293
crown 117, 252, 293
cup 53
Cupid 294

Daedalus 143
dagger 121, 245
Dalai Lama 101
dance 123
dawn 203
day and night 196–197
death 37, 42, 44, 108,
    121, 123, 137, 185,
    196, 201, 204, Tarot
    297 see also heaven; hell
Dee, John 243
Demeter 155
demon 216
Devil (Tarot) 298, 299
dharma 41
diamond 200
Diana 57 see also
    Artemis
Dionysus 56, 161, 168, 178
disease 196–197, 198
divination 245, 289,
    307–310
dog 137, 140, 300
door 128
Dorje 195
dove 118
dragon 28, 132–134,
    198, 252
dragonfly 131

draught of fishes 147
dreams 10, 75–82, 79, 103
drink 176
drum 123
Durga 225

Ea (Onnes) 152
eagle 138, 159, 184,
    277
earth 49, 52, 92, 97,
    180, 190–191,
    astrological signs 272,
    280–281
Echo 109
elements 35, 97,
    180–191, 248
elephant 149
elixir 247
Elysian Plain 231
emerald 200
Emma-o 232
endless knot 125
entwined snakes 136
Eos 42
Eucharist 45, 45
Europa, bull and 154
evergreen 167
evocation 245
eye, as geometry 96, of
    Horus 94, jaguar's
    eyes 141

fairy 199
falcon 39
famine 121
father (archetype) 21
Father Time 215
feather 44, 144
fertility 49, 173, 208–210
fire 91, 97, 180,
    184–185, 232,
    astrological signs 268,
    274–275 see also flame
firecracker 185

fish 12, 146, 147–148, 276
flame 74, 97
flaming cauldron 197
flaming sword 232 see
    also fire
fleur de lys 117
flight 143–145
flood 35
flower 173–175, fleur de
    lys 117
flute 51
fly 157
font 114
food 176–179
Fool (Tarot) 291, 302
foot 214
footprint 214
forest 167, 168
four 105, 297, crea-
    tures of Ezekiel 64,
    302, horsemen of the
    apocalypse 121,
    worlds (Kabbalah) 260
fox 139
Freud, Sigmund 17, 42, 76.
full moon 204
funerary rites, Ancient
    Egyptian 44
furnace, alchemist's
    250, 252
Fuseli, Henry 79

Gaia 164
Ganesha 25, 150
Ganges river 187
garden 164, 175, 230
garland 174
garlic 174
Garuda 159
Geb 49–50
Gemini 278–279
gemstones 198–200
geometrical shapes
    90–98
gibbet 297
gluttony 155
gnome 181

Index

Index

goat 151–153, 159, 280
God 38–39, 41, *91*, *92*,
    194, 201–*202*, *203*,
    the Father *222*, in
    Kabbalah 255, 256,
    258, 260
goddesses 27, 58, 164,
    222–227, Chinese 194,
    225, Egyptian 49, *56*,
    58, *141*, 155, 164,
    183, 273, Greek *42*,
    154, 192, *203*, 209,
    213, Indian 122, *150*,
    155–156, *227*, 304,
gods 25, 38–39, 56–57,
    220–227, 230, Aztec
    38, *227*, Chinese *177*
    Egyptian *35*, 39, *44*,
    94, *202*, 211, 284,
    Greek 22, 49, *122*,
    136, 151, *154*, 155,
    161, *163*, 168, *178*,
    182, *187*, 194, *203*,
    208, 212, Indian 25,
    41, 50, 124, 146, 155,
    159, *209*, *227*, 304,
    Norse 22–23, 151, 193,
    195, Roman *108*, *119*,
    224
gold (colour) *110*
gold (metal) 198, 199,
    200, 246–247, crown
    117
golden apple *179*, *213*
Golden Dawn system
    244–245
golden fleece *110*
good and evil 216–217
Good Shepherd *152*
green *110*, lion *250*
griffin *138*
grimoire 243
Guanyin *225*
Gurdjieff, George
    Ivanovitch 237

Hades 231
hair, locket with *212*
halo *218*
hammer *195*
hand *214*
Hanged Man (Tarot) 297
Hanuman *150*
hare *158*
harp *123*
harpy *162*
hazel 168
heart *44*, *214*
heaven 49, 52, *92*,
    230–235, *see also*
    death; hell
Heavenly Twins 278
Helios *203*
hell *92*, 230–235,
    Japanese *232*, *see also*
    death; heaven
heraldry *116*
    heraldic beasts
    137–138
herbs 173, *175*
hermaphrodite 50, *252*
Hermes 57, *136*
Hermetica 242–243
Hermit (Tarot) 295
hero 43
hieroglyphs *12*
Hierophant (Tarot) 293
High Priestess (Tarot) 292
Holy Grail *112*
Holy Spirit *87*, *118*
honey *176*
horn *123*
horoscopes, origin of 271
horse *121*, *137*
Horus 39, 211
hourglass *111*, *215*
house, and man *262*,
    House of God (Tarot)
    299
human body *96*, 173,
    180, 208, 212
hybrid creatures
    159–163

Icarus *143*
ice 188, *232*
ill omen, bird of 143
Inari *139*
incense *185*
insect 157
Isis *56*, 155, *182*, *204*
isle of the blessed,
    Celtic *110*

jackal *140*
Jacob's ladder *232*
jade *200*
jaguar's eyes *141*
Jesus *see* Christ
jewelry *158*, 198–200, *212*
Jonah and the whale *148*
Judgement (Tarot) 301
Judgement of Paris *213*
Jung, Carl Gustav
    13–17, 77, 84–85, 222,
    and alchemists *13*
    archetypes 13–23, 28,
    47, 49, gods and
    myths 38, 43
Jupiter, astrology *200*,
    276, god 57, *108*
Justice (Tarot) 295

Kabbalah 48, 255–262,
    284
Kabbalistic tree of life
    257–260, *259*
karma 216–217
king 249, 252, *see also*
    monarchy; queen
knot 124–125
Krishna *51*, 211
Kundalini 306

labyrinth 102–103, and
    the Minotaur *102*
Lakshmi 122
lamb, sacrificial *152*

lamp 116, 245
lantern 185, 295
Laozi 153
lapis lazuli 198
Lascaux cave art 32, 33
Last Supper 179
laurel 168
Leda and the swan 145
Leo (astrology) 274–275
Lévi, Eliphas 245, 245, 284
Lévi-Strauss, Claude 41
Libra 279
lightning 194
lily 117
lingam 66, 208, 209, 304
lion 138, 159, 250, 274–275
locket with hair 212
Loki 23
lotus 99, 174, 304
Lovers (Tarot) 294
Lucifer 198
lyre 123

M 107
magician 47, 228–229, 244, Tarot 291
Ma-Gu 43
male and female 49–51, 300–301, marriage 46–47, 210, sexuality 17, 205, 208–210 303–304 see also anima/animus
mandala 13, 96, 99–101, 304, meditation on 73
mandorla 219
mandrake 173
mantra 48, 99, 106, 112
Manu 41
marriage 46–47, 205, 210
Mars, astrology 200, 274, 277, god 108, 199

mask 34, 218, 221
matter and spirit 205
maypole 210
maze 102–103
meditation 71–72, 71
Medusa 136
Mercury, alchemy 249, 249, 250, 252, astrology 278, 281, god 57
mermaid 162
milk 58, and honey 176
Minotaur 102
mistletoe 174
monarchy 114–117, see also king; queen
monk 217
monkey 149–150
moon 91, 158, 201–202, 204, 248, astrology 268, 276, Tarot 300
mother (archetype) 21, 22
motherhood 156
mountain 191
Mount Meru 110, 304
mourning 110
mouse 129
mushroom 177
music 122–123
myth 38–43

nakedness 211, 302
Narcissus 109
nature 164–166
Nephthys 56
Neolithic symbolism 33–37
Neptune, astrology 276, god 189
new moon 204
night 196–197, 252
nigredo 249
Nirvana 131, 234
Noah 118, 193
Nokomis 164

numbers 104–105, 306–311, in Kabbalah 257
nurse of the gods 197
Nut (goddess) 50, 273

oak 168
occult systems 242–245
octopus 148
Oedipus 42
oil lamp 116
olive branch 118
Om 107
Om Mani Padme Hum 99
Ondine 181
opposites 52–55, 308
orb 117, 293
Orpheus 122
Osiris 44, 182
ouroboros 136
oval 94
owl 229
ox 153

pagoda 191
Paleolithic symbolism 37
palm tree 167
Pan 168
paradise 173, 230
parasol 201
Paris 179, 213
path 103, 258, 258
peace 118–119
peach 178
peacock 145
pearl 199
pelican 144
pentagram 97
Persephone 177
phallus 121, 208, phallic giant 210
philosopher's stone 247, 250

phoenix *184*
pig 131, black 155, as
  gluttony *155*
pilgrim's staff 295
pine cone *168*
Pisces (astrology) 276
pitcher 299
planets in astrology
  266–268
plants 173–175
plough (Big Dipper)
  202
Pluto 277
pomegranate *177*
Poseidon *189*
prana 183
prayer 48, wheel 112
prehistory, symbols in
  33–37
priest 229
Prometheus *186*
psychoanalysis, Jungian
  see Jung, Carl Gustav
Ptolemy 267, 270
purification rites 45
pyramid *98*

quartz 198
queen 249, 252, *see
  also* king; monarchy
Quetzalcoatl 85, *227*

Radha *51*
raft *188*
rain 36, 141, *189*
rainbow *87*, 192–193,
  193, *246*, rainbow
  body *192*
ram 274
raven *144*
rebirth 231
red *108*, 248, agate *119*,
  robe 295, rose *249*,
  ruby *200*
ring *174*

Ripley, George *254*
ritual 44–48
river *107*, *234*
robe 88, *211*, 295
Romulus and Remus 139
rosary 112
rose *174*, *249*
rosy cross *71*, *95*, *244*
ruby *200*
rue *175*

sacrifice 47, sacrificial
  lamb *152*
Sagittarius (astrology)
  275
sailing ship *182*
St Catherine of
  Alexandria 58
St Christopher 58
St Luke *147*
St Patrick *188*
St Peter *147*
salamander *181*
salmon *147*
Salome *21*
sapphire 200
Satan *28*, *92*, 141, 151,
  157, *161*, 216
Saturn, astrology 278,
  280, god 212, *224*
satyr *161*
scales *121*, 279, 295
scallop shell *146*, *205*
scarab *26*
sceptre 293
science and astrology
  267–273
Scorpio (astrology) 277
scorpion 277
sculpture 111
scythe 297
sea *161*, *163*, *189*
Seal of Solomon *97*
Selene *203*
Semele 194
serpent 166, *258*, brass

257, chimera *161*,
  guarding cave 198,
  Kundalini 306,
  ouroboros *136*,
  Quetzalcoatl *227*,
  seven-headed *135*,
  sky serpent 193, *see
  also* snake
Seth 155
seven 36, *97*, *105*,
  -headed serpent *135*
sexuality *see* male and
  female
shadow 23, *25*, *219*
Shakti 208, 304
shaman 50, *153*, 195, 213
shapes 87–89
sheaf of corn *177*
sheep 151–152
shell 146
shield 116, 137
ship burial *185*
Shiva 196, 208, *209*,
  225, *227*, 304
silken cord *125*
silver 199, *200*, crown
  117
siren *163*
sixteen regions of Hell
  (Japanese) *232*
skeleton *215*, 297
sky 108
sleep *197*
smoke *185*
snake 131, *159*, *249*
  entwined *136*, *see
  also* serpent
snow *188*
sound 105–107
sow 155, and litter *156*
sphinx *160*
spider *157*
spiral *125*
square *91*, *98*
Sri Yantra *100*, 303
stag *153*
star *140*, 202, 294, Tarot

Index

299, *see also* astrology
steam *187*
stone 248–250, circle *127*
stream *187*
Strength (Tarot) 296
stupa *97*
Styx, river *234*
sun 201, *248*, astrology *268*, 271, 274–275, disc, winged *202*, Tarot 300–301
sun shade, Buddhist *201*
swan *145*
swastika *94*
Sweat Lodge ceremony *187*
swine 155–156
sword 119, *121*, *245*, 295, fiery *232*
sylph *181*

T'aiji 50, *53*, *216*
talisman 111
tamarisk 168
Tantra 303–306
taper 302
Tarot 282–302
Tartarus 231
Taurus (astrology) 280–281
Temperance (Tarot) 298
temple 127, *127*
ten, sefirah (Kabbalah) 258–261, tetragrammaton *225*
Theseus *102*, 211
thirteen 297
Thor 151, *195*
Thoth 284
thread of life *124*
three *91*, *104*, 297, Celtic triple enclosure 98, fates *124*, fishes *12*, *147*, magi *104*, mystic monkeys *149*

realms *92*, triple cross 293, triple lily *117*
throne *115*
Thunderbird 194
thyme *175*
Tian Mu 194
tiger *142*
Tir Nan Og (Celtic isle of the blessed) *110*
toad *159*, 229
toadstool 177
tomb *127*
totem pole *37*
Tower (Tarot) 299
treasure *127*
tree 143, 166, 167–172, of life 143, *153*, *170*, *187*, 257–260, *258*
triangle 89, *91*, *92*, *97*, 99
trickster (archetype) 22
Trinity *104*, *147*
Tristram and Iseult 49
trumpet 301
Tsitigarbha *231*
two, Heavenly Twins 278–279, realms *52*

unicorn *138*
Uranus, astrology 278, god *146*

Vajravarahi 155–156
Valhalla 231
valley *191*
vampire bats 197
Venus, astrology 279, 280, goddess 57, *146*, 153, sculptures 37, 111
violet *109*
Virgin, Mary 56, 166, 198, Mother *174*, as Queen of Heaven *109*
Virgo (astrology) 281

Vishnu *41*, *51*, 146, *148*, 156, *159*
volcano *191*

Waite Tarot pack 284–285
wand 302
war *108*, 118–121
water *91*, *92*, *97*, *109*, 176, 180, 187–189, astrological signs 272, 276–277
water-carrier 278
waxing moon *204*
Way of Truth *103*
weapons of war *121*
wedding cake *210*
well *187*
werewolf *140*, 197
wheel, of Fortune (Tarot) 296, of life, Buddhist *93*
white *110*, 248–249, bull 153–154, elephant *149*, rose 249, sow *156*
window *128*
wine *45*, *176*, *178*
witch 228–229
wizard 228–229
wolf 22, 139, *140*

Yama, lord of death *93*
yantra 99–101
yellow 25, *109*
Yijing 307–311
yin-yang *189*, *216*
yoni 304

Zammurrad 25
zero 302
Zeus 57, 151, *154*, 155, 194
zodiac 263–281

ACKNOWLEDGMENTS

The publishers wish to thank the following photographers and organizations for their kind permission to reproduce the copyright material in this book.

KEY: t: top, b: bottom, c: centre, l: left, r: right

AA: The Art Archive, London
AA&A: Ancient Art & Architecture
        Collection, Pinner
BAL: Bridgeman Art Library, London
BL: British Library, London
BM: British Museum, London
CWC: Charles Walker Collection, Yorkshire
MEPL: Mary Evans Picture Library, London
MH: Michael Holford, Loughton
V&A: Victoria and Albert Museum, London

Page 1 CWC; **7b** CWC; **8** The Eagle and Snake, Tibetan *thangka*, Private Collection; **10–11** Francis I guides the Ship of France drawn by the White Hind, 1515, from *Codex Guelf* 86.4. The Ducal Library, Wolfenbuttel/ Weidenfeld & Nicolson Archive, London; **12l** BL; **13** CWC; **20** Jan Croot Collection; **21** Museo Diocesano de Barcelona/BAL; **22–23** Musee des Beaux Arts, Chartes/BAL; **24** MH; **28** CWC; **29** The goddess Amaterasu, The Japanese Gallery, London/ DBP Archive; **32–33** Colorphoto Hans Hinz, Basel; **34** BM/BAL; **35t** Werner Forman Archive, London; **35b** V&A/BAL; **37** Hanz Schmied, Z.E.F.A.; **38** Bibliotheque de l'Assemblee Nationale Francaise, Paris; **40** BL/BAL; **43** BL/MH; **44** BM/MH; **45** V&A/AA; **49** CWC; **50–51** V&A/MH; **52** CWC; **54–55** The Tate Gallery, London; **56** Werner Forman Archive, London; **57** Huis Bergh Collection/CWC; **59** Barry Friedman, New York/BAL; **63** Fitzwilliam Museum, University of Cambridge; **64** Trier Cathedral, Germany/AA; **69** V&A/AA; **72** V&A/ BAL; **78** Goethe Museum, Frankfurt/Colorphoto Hans Hinz, Basel; **83** Private Collection; **88–89** Turkish and Islamic Art Museum, Istanbul/AA; **93** Robert Bere Collection, Oxford; **96t** AA&A; **96b** Dar al Athar al Islammiyyah, Kuwait/CWC; **100** Private Collection; **101** Private Collection/ MH; **102t** Chartres Cathedral, France/CWC; **102c** Palazzo Ducale, Mantua/ AA&A; **104** CWC; **113** Musee Conde, Chantilly/BAL; **116** The College of Arms, London; **119** CWC; **120** Private Collection/BAL; **122** Hatay Museum, Antioch/ Sonia Halliday Photographs; **124** MEPL; **125tl** Southwark Cathedral, London/ AA&A, Pinner; **126** Biblioteca Estense, Modena/AA; **128t** V&A/BAL;

130 V&A/AA; **133** Richardson and Kailas Icons, London/BAL; **137** Civic Library, Padua/AA; **138** National Library of Scotland, Edinburgh/ BAL; **139** Private Collection; **140r** Ann Ronan Picture Library, London; **142t** BL; **143** MEPL; **145t** Uffizi, Florence/BAL, London; **146** Uffizi, Florence/BAL; **148b** MEPL; **150t** V&A/BAL; **150b** CWC; **153b** Private Collection; **154t** Museo de Bellas Artes, Bilbao/ BAL; **156t** Private Collection; **158b** Private Collection; **162–163b** BL/BAL; **165** V&A; **171bl** Private Collection; **172b** Real Biblioteca de El Escorial, Madrid/Oronoz; **173** CWC; **175t** Private Collection; **175b** Bodleian Library, Oxford/ BAL; **176** Aberdeen University Library/ BAL; **179** Church of Our Lady of the Pastures, Asinov/Sonia Halliday Photographs, Buckinghamshire; **182b** Private Collection, Lamberhurst; **186** Prado, Madrid/BAL; **189** Private Collection; **190t** Private Collection, Lamberhurst; **198** Natural History Museum, London; **199t & b** Judy Garlick Curio Collection; **200t & bl** Spink and Son, London; **200r** Private Collection; **207** The Bible Society, London/BAL; **210t** MEPL; **211** Private Collection; **212–213** Prado, Madrid/BAL; **215t** Bodleian Library, Oxford/AA; **215b** Private Collection; **216b** CWC; **217t** Bibliotheque Nationale, Paris/BAL; **217b** Private Collection, Lamberhurst; **218b** Biblioteca Capitolare, Vercelli/AA; **219b** Municipal Library, Mantua/AA; **220–221** Tony Morrison/South American Pictures, Woodbridge; **222–223** Ducal Library, Wolfenbuttel/ Weidenfeld & Nicolson Archive, London; **224** Ann Ronan Picture Library, London; **226–227** Private Collection; **229** CWC; **230** Johnny van Haeften Gallery, London/BAL; **232t** MEPL; **233** Horniman Museum, London/AA; **234b** Prado, Madrid/BAL; **235** Cellarius: Orbits of the Planets, 1668, BL; **237** Private Collection; **241** V&A/AA; **242** CWC; **243** CWC; **244** AA&A; **246** CWC; **247** CWC; **248–249** CWC; **250** CWC; **251** CWC; **253** CWC; **254** CWC; **256** CWC; **259** CWC; **261** Illustration by Caroline Church/Garden Studio; **262** CWC; **263** CWC; **266** Ann Ronan Picture Library, London; **269** Biblioteca Estense, Modena/AA; **270–271** BL/AA; **273** BM/MH; **283** CWC; **284–285** CWC; **290–302** BM; **305** Gulbenkian Museum, Durham/ John Webb; **309** CWC; **310** CWC.

COMMISSIONED ARTWORK CREDITS
Commissioned illustrations by
Hannah Firmin/Sharp Practice.